Y0-CDN-747

DATA ADMINISTRATION

William Durell

DATA ADMINISTRATION

A Practical Guide to Successful Data Management

McGraw-Hill Book Company

New York St. Louis San Francisco Auckland Bogotá Hamburg Johannesburg London Madrid Mexico Montreal New Delhi Panama Paris São Paulo Singapore Sydney Tokyo Toronto

Library of Congress Cataloging in Publication Data

Durell, William.
Data Administration.

Bibliography: p.
Includes index.
1. Data Base Management. I. Title.
QA76.9.D3D87 1985 001.64'4 84-11200
ISBN 0-07-018391-0

1 2 3 4 5 6 7 8 9 0 DOC/DOC 8 9 8 7 6 5 4

0-07-018391-0

The editors for this book were Tyler G. Hicks and Stephan Owen Parnes, the designer was Elliot Epstein, and the production supervisor was Teresa F. Leaden. It was set in Baskerville by Monotype Composition Company, Inc.

Printed and bound by R. R. Donnelley & Sons Company

This book is devoted to data administration
—an island of discipline in an ocean of disorder.

CONTENTS

3 STANDARDS, POLICIES, AND PROCEDURES FOR DATA USE 31

4 DATA ADMINISTRATION ACTIVITIES: WHY, WHAT, WHEN, AND HOW 121

5 DATA ADMINISTRATION: TOPICAL AREAS 167

FOREWORD

During the early years of data processing, we lacked a rigorous, disciplined approach to the development of data processing systems. Thus, the methods we used to design automated systems were intuitive rather than systematic. Structured analysis and design techniques promoted by Yourdon, Constantine, DeMarco, Myers, and others have since provided us with a scientific approach to process or program design. However, until recently there has been little research and development concerning a scientific approach to the design and management of data structures. The design of data need not, and should not, be an intuitive process. The information resources of your enterprise are too valuable not to be managed and controlled by scientific means. The rules, guidelines, and examples within this book will provide you with the knowledge necessary to transform the *art* of data design into the *science* of data design.

ACKNOWLEDGMENTS

I would like to thank Robert N. Whitaker for planting the seed of imagination that has led me to write this book. Special thanks are due to Mark E. Lipp and Paul L. Williams for generously donating their valuable time to review the manuscript and provide their critique. I greatly appreciate the words of encouragement from relatives, friends, and business associates during the production of this book.

PREFACE

The purpose of this book is to help transform the *art* of data administration into the *science* of data administration. This book is an attempt to introduce more practicality into a field that is overburdened with concept and theory. This book does not contain solutions for every problem of information resource management, nor does it cover all aspects of data administration. However, it does provide both concrete examples and solutions to many of the day-to-day problems encountered by data administrators.

It is my hope that this book will inspire others to write books on the practical application of data administration. If it achieves nothing else, it will still be a success.

THE MYTH OF DATA DICTIONARIES

A basic assumption among some new and potential dictionary users is that once a dictionary is installed, it somehow automatically provides instant control and benefits to the information management activities of an enterprise.

While a dictionary can allow a user to effectively manage his data resource, it requires a significant amount of planning and preparation before it can be put into production. If an enterprise does not understand how or elects not to implement a dictionary system correctly, the results achieved will fall far below expectations.

THE INFANCY OF DATA ADMINISTRATION

During the early years of data processing, it was believed that automation could reduce the cost and improve the accuracy of any manual or clerical procedure. The computer was touted as a panacea for all of the ills of a business. Little thought was given to determining which applications should be computerized and in which sequence. Priorities for system development were assigned according to the decibel level of the users screaming for data processing services.

We soon realized that not every manual process could become a cost-effective automated one. The profitability of data processing systems, as with any company asset, must be measured in terms of return on investment (ROI). A company should clearly document ROI before undertaking any system development project, whether large or small.

The learning process during the infancy of data processing reflects an increase in understanding about the ROI of system development. Data processors have developed several tools to assist them in documenting a systems ROI. Cost-benefit analysis, feasibility studies, and benchmark tests are all ways to measure the cost-effectiveness of hardware and software.

Data administration and information resource management are relative newcomers to the field of data processing. It has only been within the last five years that the data processing industry has given serious consideration to the management and control of information as a corporate resource.

We are experiencing a learning process in data administration similar to the learning process during the infancy of the data processing industry. A popular notion today among many data processors and data administrators is that we should load any and every available piece of information into a data dictionary. The dictionary is expected to magically cure all of our information ills. The fallacy of this is the same as that of automating any and every manual procedure. Many data processing shops have learned the hard way that not all information management projects make cost-effective dictionary applications. There are quantifiable costs and benefits associated with all dictionary and data administration endeavors.

The purpose of this book is to provide answers to the following questions:

- What are the costs and benefits of data administration?
- Which projects make cost-justifiable data dictionary applications and which do not?
- How can a company maximize its return on investment from data administration?

Chapter 1

WHAT IS DATA ADMINISTRATION?

WHAT IS A DATA DICTIONARY?

Since the data dictionary is an integral part of data administration (DA), it is important to understand the concept of data dictionary/directory systems before explaining the overall concepts of data administration.

There is nothing magical or mystical about a data dictionary. In fact, the concept of a data dictionary, when compared to other data processing concepts, is a surprisingly simple one. A data dictionary is simply a mechanism to collect, maintain, and publish information about data. It is a central repository of *metadata* (information about data).

Basically, a data dictionary provides a mechanism to define and use information about data elements, groups of elements (records or segments), groups of records (files or databases), and the relationships between these entities. It is also capable of defining other entities, such as input forms, reports, screens, processes, procedures, and just about anything else. However, all data definition entities are built on the foundation of the element definition. Figure 1-1 is an example of an element definition. The definition in Figure 1-1 provides answers to the following questions about this particular piece of data:

- What is the name of this piece of data? (ELEMENT NAME)
- Who created this definition? (OWNED BY)
- When was the definition created? (ENCODED)
- Under what name is this data referenced in a COBOL program? (COBOL ALIAS)

ELEMENT NAME:	US-POSTAL-STATE-CODE
OWNED BY:	Accounts Payable Department
ENCODED:	02 JUL 81 AT 15:13
ALIASES/SYNONYMS:	
	COBOL: US-POSTAL-STATE-CODE IMS: STCODE
CATALOGED AS:	US STATE CODE POSTAL ST CD
DESCRIPTION:	The standard alphabetic state abbreviation used by the U.S. Postal Service.
NOTE:	These codes are used to validate the state in the vendor's mailing address. This alphabetic code is matched against the payroll system state numeric tax code in the payroll-system STATE-TABLE.
VALID VALUES:	AK = Alaska AL = Alabama AZ = Arizona AR = Arkansas CA = California CO = Colorado CT = Connecticut DE = Delaware DC = District of Columbia FL = Florida GA = Georgia HI = Hawaii . . . . . . VI = Virgin Islands
FORMAT:	Alphanumeric 2

Fig. 1-1 Sample contents of data dictionary.

- Under what name is this data referenced in IMS? (IMS ALIAS)
- How is it possible to perform an automated search for this data element in the dictionary? (CATALOGED AS)
- What is the definition of this piece of data? (DESCRIPTION)
- What is the relationship of this data to other data? (NOTE)
- How is this element validated? (VALID VALUES)
- In what format and length is this data stored? (FORMAT)

Data dictionaries are often identified as data dictionary/directory systems (DD/DS). That is, these systems are capable of not only storing metadata (data dictionary), but are also capable of providing cross-reference information (directory) about the metadata. The dictionary provides information (such as that in Figure 1-1) about what the data is and how it is used. Thus, the dictionary often provides a *logical* view of the data. The directory provides information about where it physically resides and how it can be accessed. For example, the directory could provide answers to the following questions:

- What programs use US-POSTAL-STATE-CODE?
- What records or segments contain the data element US-POSTAL-STATE-CODE?

THE DATA ADMINISTRATION IDENTITY PROBLEM

Even among experienced data processing staff members, there is a lack of understanding of the purpose and objectives of data administration. When asked what data administration is, the answer provided by a programmer or an analyst will typically fall into two categories:

- Data administration has something to do with data dictionaries.
- Data administration has something to do with data bases.

While these answers are not incorrect, they merely describe some of the tools or facilities used by data administration. They do not adequately define the purpose of DA.

Databases and data dictionaries are resources and tools available to the data administrator, but they are only a means to an overall objective. The overall objective of DA is to plan, document, manage, and control the information resources of an entire organization. Data dictionaries and databases help us achieve this goal, but neither is an end in itself. The role of data administration is not to maintain individual databases and dictionaries. The role of DA is to integrate and manage corporation-wide information resources *by utilizing* data dictionaries and well-designed data structures.

WHAT IS DATA ADMINISTRATION, AND WHY DO WE NEED IT?

To better explain the concept of data administration, let us discuss some of the questions most commonly raised concerning the nature and purpose of DA.

Question: We already have a data dictionary, why do we need data administration?

Compiling all of the information described in Figure 1-1 for all the data elements in an organization would involve considerable expenditures of time and money. Without proper planning and coordination, an organization will realize a low return from this investment. To maximize the return on investment from a data dictionary, data administration must provide management with answers to the following questions:

1. What will be achieved by implementing a data dictionary? What are the costs and benefits associated with its implementation?
2. What information should be loaded into the data dictionary?
3. Who will be responsible for inputting information into the dictionary?
4. Who must review and approve this information before it is entered in the dictionary?
5. What steps will be taken to insure the quality of information before it is entered?
6. Once information is loaded into the dictionary, how will it be maintained?
7. Who is responsible for maintaining the integrity of the data in the dictionary?
8. Will the dictionary be used for developing new systems or for assistance in maintaining existing systems?
9. Which software languages will be supported by the dictionary?
10. What database management systems will the dictionary support?
11. Will this dictionary be used by the entire organization, by individual departments, or individual application development projects? Should the data dictionary be used to document data or process definitions, or both?
12. Who will be the end users of the dictionary?
13. What training will be necessary for users of the dictionary?
14. What will be the first project or application using the dictionary?
15. In what sequence should other projects or applications be added?
16. What are the short- and long-term objectives of using the data dictionary?
17. Does management understand all of the capabilities and facilities of the dictionary?

The objective of data administration is to answer these and many other questions before a data dictionary is implemented. By doing so, an organization can assure itself that the implementation of a dictionary will be sensible and cost-effective.

Question: We already have database administrators, why do we need data administration?

Normally, database administrators are responsible only for the design, implementation, security, and maintenance of physical databases. It is the responsibility of data administration (DA) to determine the contents and boundaries of each database. DA first builds a logical model of the database which is later implemented by database administration (DBA). This is analogous to the distinction between a systems analyst and a systems designer. But before DA and DBA can design a single logical and physical database, DA should strive to plan and coordinate the construction of all new databases throughout an organization. DA should provide answers to the following questions:

1. How many new databases are planned for development over the next *n* years?
2. Will the implementation of these data structures support the long-range goals of the business systems plan or other business requirements of the organization?
3. How can these databases be constructed to minimize the redundancy of information among databases?
4. What communications will be required among databases?
5. In what sequence should these databases be implemented?

In other words, data administration should develop a business systems plan for data usage throughout an organization. If physical database systems are built without regard to an overall plan, the databases will reflect the same data incompatibilities, inconsistencies, and redundancies of the data structures they are replacing. Figure 1-2 illustrates the differences in the responsibilities of DA and DBA.

Question: Programmers and analysts have always managed data; why do we need data administration for this?

Analysts and programmers have managed only those data structures for the systems and programs under their individual control. This piecemeal management has led to a proliferation of data redundancy and incompatibility of data among programs and systems.

	Data administration	Database administration
Primary responsibility	Administrative	Technical
Scope	All databases	Database specific
Data design	Logical	Physical
Primary liaison	Management	Programmers, analysts
Range of concern	Long-term data planning	More concerned with short-term development and use of databases
Primary orientation	Metadata data dictionary data analysis DBMS independent	Data Database Data design Database management systems specific

Fig. 1-2 Comparison of responsibilities of data administration and database administration.

Users are now demanding comprehensive data processing systems whose data spans many applications and organizational boundaries. For example, the personnel department now expects access to data that was formerly the private property of the payroll department. Likewise, the payroll department would like to be privy to personnel-related employee information. This requires the creation of a comprehensive payroll-personnel employee database. The coordination and planning required for the successful implementation of this comprehensive data structure can only be achieved by a top-down approach. Data administration must be a leader in this effort.

THE DATA ADMINISTRATION CHARTER

Because data administration is a relatively new concept to data processing, it is important to document the objectives and scope of DA within the organization. This document should be reviewed and approved by both data processing and end-user management. The DA charter should provide answers to the following questions:

1. How will the DA staff be organized?
2. What are the job descriptions of the members of the DA staff?
3. What level of expertise is needed for DA staff members?
4. What are the accountabilities and responsibilities of DA?

5. What will be the relationship between the DA and data processing organizations?
6. What will be the relationship between the DA and end-user departments?
7. What is the relationship between DA and database administration?
8. What are the short- and long-range goals of DA?

Chapter 2

SELLING DATA ADMINISTRATION TO YOUR ORGANIZATION

BENEFITS OF DATA ADMINISTRATION

Short-Term versus Long-Term Benefits

The traditional development of information systems within an organization has followed a piecemeal, single-application–single-project scenario. Likewise, a series of data structures have been constructed to support a series of single applications. For example, if a company is interested in developing a payroll system to eliminate the need for an outside service bureau to print paychecks, it will build a payroll application with a data store containing employee payroll–related information. This is illustrated in Figure 2-1. As the company grows and the number of employees increases, the company adds a personnel application to its information systems. To minimize the cost and time needed to develop this system, it is decided that a separate data structure will be built to accommodate the data required by the personnel system. Of course, interface software must be built to pass personnel information to the payroll system and to pass any required information from the payroll system to the personnel system. This interface software also performs checks and balances and prints audit trails to help assure that the data within the payroll data stores is consistent with the personnel system data. These interface requirements are illustrated in Figure 2-2.

As the company grows and adds more employees, an employee tracking–job history system is added to provide the personnel department with available information concerning employee skills, education, and work experience. To minimize the short-term cost and time span of the project, it is decided not to integrate job history data into either

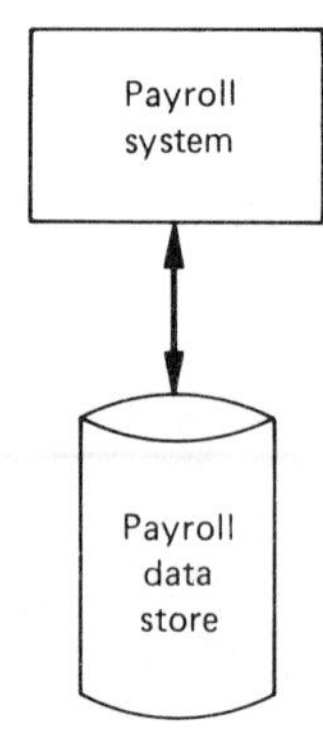

Fig. 2-1 Single system–single data store interface.

the payroll or personnel data stores. A separate job history database is built to store the data required for this new application. Of course, additional interface programs are required to attempt to keep the payroll, personnel, and job history data stores reasonably consistent. As the company grows and the number of employees increases, a labor distribution system is needed to more closely account for labor costs in the various areas of the company. To minimize the short-term project costs, a labor distribution software package is purchased. Since this software package has its own database, additional interface programs must be written to link this data with that of the payroll, personnel, and job history systems.

The results of the piecemeal construction of four independent sets of data structures is illustrated in Figure 2-3. This human resource

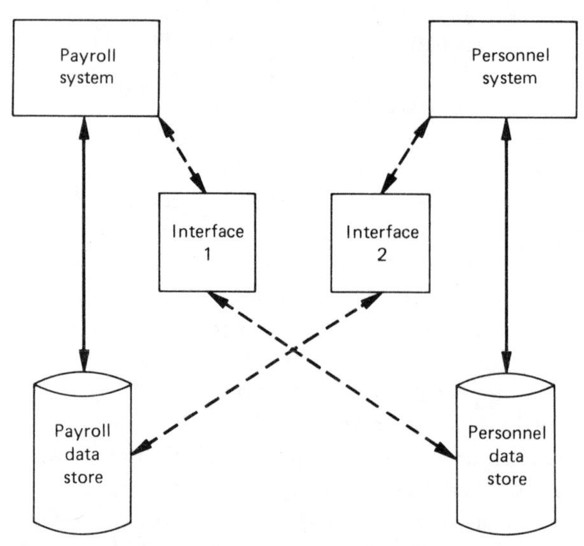

Fig. 2-2 Interfaces with two systems and two data stores.

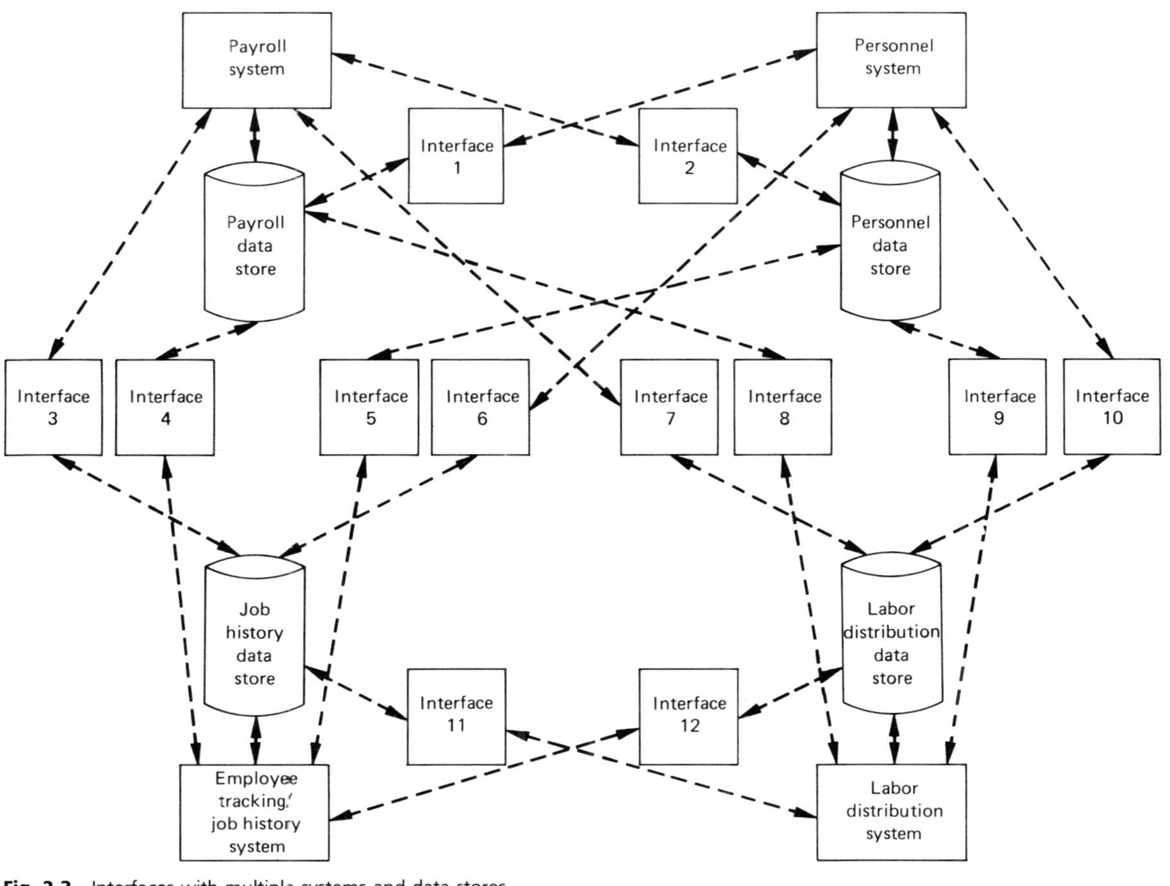

Fig. 2-3 Interfaces with multiple systems and data stores.

Number of Applications	Number of Data Stores	Possible Number of Interfaces
1	1	0
2	2	1
3	3	6 (3 × 2)
4	4	12 (4 × 3)
5	5	20 (5 × 4)
6	6	30 (6 × 5)
7	7	42 (7 × 6)

Fig. 2-4 Possible number of interfaces.

information system has become a complex web of complicated and redundant data stores. It is now extremely difficult and expensive to modify or expand any part of this system. This is because of the high incidence of redundant or overlapping data that is stored and transferred from application to application.

Let us assume that each application has only one data store (typically,

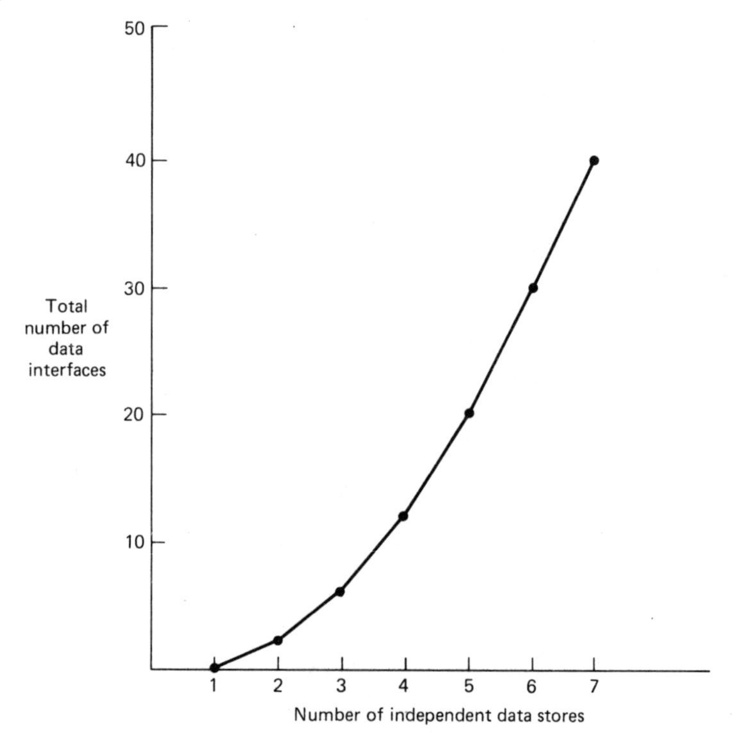

Fig. 2-5 Cost of nonintegrated data.

there are several redundant data sets used within a single application). Figure 2-4 demonstrates the additional interface requirements as additional application systems and data stores are linked together. The number and complexity of these interfaces grows geometrically with each new application. The cost of each new system can be directly correlated to the complexity involved. This is illustrated in Figure 2-5. Eventually, the cost to add additional applications, and to integrate them with existing applications, becomes prohibitive.

One role of data administration is to advocate the planning and coordination of the information resource across related applications. By doing so, the amount of data sharing can be maximized, and the amount of data redundancy minimized. Figure 2-6 illustrates an integrated human resource system that shares employee information among all related applications. Figure 2-7 demonstrates the long-term benefits of the comprehensive planning for the global use of the information resource. The relative high cost indicated for the development of the payroll system includes the long-term planning for all employee-related data. By doing so, all follow-on systems can utilize this comprehensive employee database. The database designed for the payroll system is designed to easily accommodate the additional data required for the other systems in the future. As the other systems are developed or rewritten to share this comprehensive employee database, the additional cost incurred is incremental, not geometric. This is because we have minimized the need for replicated data and interface software.

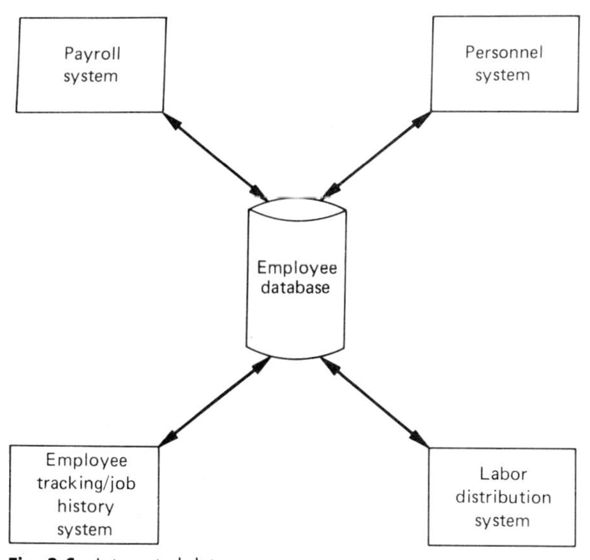

Fig. 2-6 Integrated data.

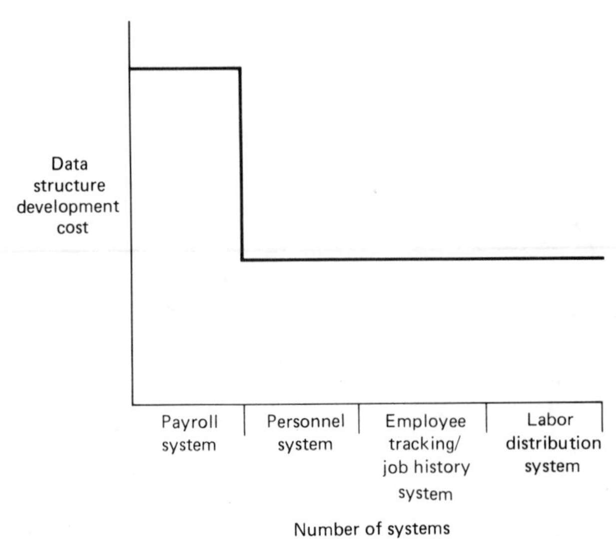

Fig. 2-7 Cost of integrated data.

Logical Data Structure Design

During the early years of the data processing industry, computers had very limited speed and storage capacity. Accordingly, programs and systems were designed to maximize the limited resources of the CPU and to minimize the internal storage space consumed. However, as the cost of hardware rapidly decreased and the cost of data processing labor increased, there has been a corresponding change in the way application systems are designed. The primary concern now is to increase the life span or modularity of programs in order to minimize future labor maintenance costs to software. Of secondary concern are the computer resources used by these programs. Thus, we have made a transition from software that optimized the hardware resource to software that optimized the labor resource. There has been considerable research and development to assist us in this transition, including the structured analysis and design concepts promoted by Yourdon, Constantine, De Marco, and Myers.

However, until very recently, there has been no measurable transition in the design of data structures. Many data structures today are designed to optimize the operating systems, the database management systems, or the hardware on which the data structures reside. As with program or process design, there are practices, principles, and standards to improve the design of data structures. These design practices can increase the life span of data structures and reduce the future maintenance costs of changes to the data structures and to the programs that use this data. Data modeling and data normalization techniques can assist us in making the transition from hardware-oriented data structures to data structures that minimize labor costs. The role of DA is to utilize these techniques and to educate and sell others on the virtues and benefits of these techniques.

Benefits to the Data Processing Department

The data processing department is the main beneficiary of the information and services provided by DA. Below is a description of some of the more important services provided by DA.

1. *Centralized control and management of data definitions* DA should be the central repository and control mechanism for all data definitions used by the application development and system maintenance staff. All additions to, changes of, and deletions from data definitions used by application programs and database management systems should be managed by DA. This management includes the security, backup, recovery, and audit trail of all changes to data definitions. By centralizing the control of this information, problems with duplicate or conflicting updates of data definitions can be minimized.

2. *Change control* DA provides the formal documentation and approval process for all changes to metadata and data definitions. By placing this control within the DA organization no changes can be made to entries in the data dictionary or to data definitions in source code libraries (COPYLIB, PANVALET, LIBRARIAN, among others) without the knowledge and consent of DA. It is also the responsibility of DA to assess the impact of any of these changes. By doing so, DA can notify all affected personnel about an impending change to the format of a data definition or data structure. This will minimize the possibility of any conflicts between actual format of the data, and that expected by the programs that use this data.

3. *Source of data-design expertise* Logical database design is a specialty that requires its own specialists. The primary responsibility of the data analyst is to perform logical data structure design or to train, advise, and assist other members of the data processing staff concerning the analysis and design of data structures. These data structures include parameter tables, files, databases, records, and segments. The knowledge of DA staff members concerning logical data design and normalization techniques is a valuable resource to the organization.

4. *Coordination of data usage* The database analyst or application development programmer or analyst is responsible for the design and/or maintenance of individual data structures. However, data administration staff members are often involved in the planning and design of data at a higher level. This broader perspective of data often spans multiple applications or databases, and sometimes spans the data resources of the entire organization. DA can provide the knowledge necessary for the effective coordination and sharing of information across organizational, project, or individual database boundaries. This minimizes data redundancy and increases the degree of data sharing among the entire organization.

The need for the coordination of data usage throughout an organization is an ever-increasing one. Gone are the days when the application development shop can design single-application, "standalone" systems. Each year, the end user gains more experience and knowledge of data processing. This increases the number and sophistication of the requests for information to be provided by data processing. Also, each year the competition increases among companies to provide ever-increasing information services to the general public. This requires more sophisticated, multiapplication, data processing systems. This demands the centralized planning, coordination, and control of the data resources used by these comprehensive systems. Without the advice and support of DA from a global viewpoint, the application development staff alone cannot handle this coordination.

Benefits to the End User

The ever-increasing need for data processing services, coupled with the limited supply and increasing expense of data processing expertise, demands that more and more traditional DP responsibilities be delegated to the end user. Distributed processing, personal computers, report-writer and query languages, and information centers have all been developed because of the need to utilize the end-user resource. However, without access to the centralized corporate information resource, these tools are of limited value. The end user must not only have access to the data itself, but must also have access to information (or metadata) about this data resource. Before being able to use the information resource effectively, an end user must understand the format and characteristics of the data and the nature of the relationships among the various pieces of data to be examined. For example, if the personnel department is to effectively utilize the data contained in the corporate payroll master file, the personnel department must be provided with information about the data on this master file. This information may include answers to the following questions:

1. How current is this data?
2. By whom is it updated?
3. What is the relationship or compatibility of this data to the employee data on the personnel system files?
4. What levels of security are placed on this data? Specifically, what information can the personnel department access and/or update?
5. What is the format of the data on an employee's record?
6. How many different types of records are associated with an employee?
7. How is the data on this file sequenced? Employee-number sequence? Social security-number sequence, division or department sequence?
8. How can data be accessed about a particular employee? Employee social security number, payroll number, or employee number?

This information about data (or metadata) is compiled and maintained by data administration. One of the most important benefits of DA is to share this metadata with the user community.

Because of the lack of standards and consistency, the infancy of the data processing industry can accurately be described as a state of disorder. Each analyst designed systems using techniques different from those of other analysts. Programmers tended to code each program in a unique way. There was little discipline and consistency, thus our systems tended to be fragmented, complicated, and expensive to maintain. When compared to the other fields of applied science, the early years of DP lacked standardization in the way we applied these tools to our jobs. Also, because of the rapid advances in technology, data processors were overwhelmed with the number and variety of tools at their disposal. This also contributed to the lack of uniformity.

Although data processors have always had many tools to do their jobs, it is only recently that we have begun to consistently apply tools and techniques to accomplish our objectives. Great gains have been made in the consistency and rigorousness with which these tools are applied to the development of data processing systems. Analysts and designers in most organizations are expected to follow company guidelines to insure the development of modular, flexible, table-driven application systems. Today, the typical data processing shop has rigorous standards for programmers to follow, to assure that programming products are consistent and cohesive.

Considerable improvements have been made in the disciplined way that application programs are designed and coded. However, these gains have been primarily in the area of program or process definition. There is still a lack of discipline concerning the effective utilization of the raw materials of processes, the raw material of data.

BENEFITS OF A DATA DICTIONARY

Although there has been an increase in the efficiency of methods used to collect, compute, and disseminate data, there is still a void in the understanding of the characteristics and relationships of the data itself. It would be unreasonable to expect an engineer or contractor to construct a high-quality building without understanding the characteristics of the building materials. Yet data processors are attempting to build high-quality systems while ignoring the characteristics of the raw material of data. Only recently has there been an interest in methods of defining and documenting information about this raw material. We have also just begun to develop the means to use this data effectively, efficiently, and consistently. The data dictionary is a tool for the effective utilization of data.

Information about Data—A Corporate Asset

Almost everyone will agree that the data compiled about a company is indeed an important corporate asset. Accurate information about how a company functions and about its employees and clients is vital to the success of any corporation. It is not difficult to measure the value of such data. According to the findings of a recent survey, only two out of ten companies whose data centers were destroyed were still in existence one year after the catastrophe. Any sensible data center will take great precautions to safeguard the company's data. Should similar precautions also be taken concerning information about our data? If a company's documentation library is destroyed by a catastrophe, what impact would this have on the survivability of this company?

Some data processing centers experience a personnel turnover rate of 100 percent every four or five years. Does it represent a catastrophe if these employees leave without documenting their knowledge of the company's data and systems? By storing this knowledge on the magnetic medium of a data dictionary and providing adequate backup and recovery for the dictionary, a corporation can safeguard against the catastrophe of data documentation destruction.

Public versus Private Information

Many data processors have written unstructured, spaghetti programs. The program code contained many branches and switches and as a result was extremely complicated. The primary goal was to streamline code so that source program storage space and processing time could be conserved. It was a source of pride to be able to process data in the least possible number of instructions. Efficiency of the code was paramount; simplicity and maintainability of the code was of secondary significance.

Each program tended to become the *Mona Lisa* of the programmer who coded it. The knowledge of how the program worked was the private property of the author, because the logic could not be easily understood and shared with other programmers. Even the author usually lost considerable insight into the code several months after it was written. Thus the programs of yesteryear were very difficult and expensive to maintain.

Then along came structured programming techniques. The concept was to code a program in such a way as to make the logic path easy to follow and easy to read. The program was more easily understood by many people, thus easier to maintain. Programs no longer were the private property of the author, because the logic could be shared with other programmers. The code became the public property of the entire programming staff. For this reason, structured programs were sometimes referred to as egoless programs. A valid comparison can be made between structured programs and a data dictionary.

The knowledge that a programmer or analyst has about a company's data and systems has tended to be the private property of each individual. Knowledge should not be inaccessible to others. It belongs on a data dictionary so that it can be accessed and shared with all members of our organization. After all, if employees are being paid to become proficient in the knowledge of the company, should they not divulge this knowledge resource to everyone? Shouldn't knowledge be the public property of the corporation? If structured programs are egoless, doesn't a data dictionary represent egoless knowledge?

It is not difficult to identify those staff members who possess the most knowledge of our data and systems. We often see these experienced people answering questions from less knowledgeable staff members. How much time and money is wasted by these employees providing answers to the same questions over and over again? Many of these questions result from a lack of understanding or documentation about the data and process entities used in the operations of an organization. By providing public access to our knowledge of these entities via the data dictionary, we can save a considerable amount of the time consumed in question-and-answer sessions.

The Data Dictionary as a Communications Tool

The shaded area in Figure 2-8 represents the communications among the departments of a large company. Traditionally, this communication

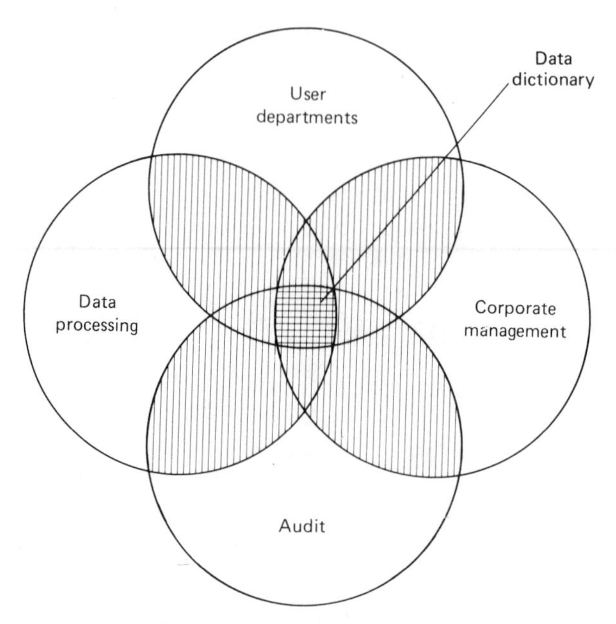

Fig. 2-8 Data dictionary as communication tool.

has taken the form of conversations, meetings, and telephone calls. This communication typically has been documented in the form of memos, meeting minutes, and notes. Occasionally, we have developed manuals and reference texts. But the value of this medium has been limited in updating capabilities and circulation techniques. In the past, what we lacked was a central pool of information that could be shared by all departments. The crosshatched area of Figure 2-8 represents the communications value of a data dictionary. The data dictionary is a central repository of information that can be accessed by all areas of a company. Unlike the traditional means of communicating by memo or other paper formats, the data dictionary is not limited to a specific distribution list. Anyone with a terminal and knowledge of the dictionary has access to all of its information.

The Data Dictionary as a Glossary of Definitions

Another use of the data dictionary is as a glossary of terms. Many employees would not consider their office to be complete without a Webster's dictionary. In many ways, the data dictionary is not unlike Webster's; it contains a glossary of terms used by the firm. If Webster's dictionary is essential to clear communication in the English language, isn't a data dictionary essential for clear communication within the corporation? As a glossary of terms, the data dictionary can be an invaluable education tool for new employees in data processing and user areas.

The Data Dictionary as a System Development and Maintenance Tool

The data dictionary can be a very effective tool to support structured analysis and design. It can be used to document data store, data flow, and process entity types. As such, it is an efficient way of portraying system design details to the user.

The data dictionary can also be used to generate file, segment, and record definitions for a variety of programming languages. By doing so, we can centralize the control of program data definitions. This will ensure consistency of data use and inhibit data redundancy.

Because we can centralize control of data use, the data dictionary can be a very effective tool in change-control management. Since the data dictionary is the origin of all data definitions, any new data requirements must have the knowledge and approval of data administration.

Because the dictionary enforces consistency of data naming and format variation, it significantly reduces the cost of program maintenance. Many of us have experienced system maintenance requests involving the expansion of certain data elements. Payroll numbers, account numbers, and zip codes are prime examples. Before we convert our systems to handle a nine-digit zip code, wouldn't it be beneficial to be able to use a data dictionary to identify every occurrence of POSTAL-ZIP-CODE?

Impact Analysis and Estimating

Because the dictionary allows us to more accurately identify where data is used, it can improve the accuracy in assessing the impact of a change in the design of data.

For example, suppose a company is expanding CUSTOMER-ACCT-NBR from 8 to 12 positions. What impact will this have on the general ledger, accounts payable, and accounts receivable systems? Using the data dictionary, we can identify all programs that use CUSTOMER-ACCT-NBR. We can also identify which data definitions are affected by this change. Thus the dictionary provides us with more information to accurately assess and estimate the costs involved in making a change in the design of data.

The Data Dictionary as a Superior Documentation Medium

Traditionally, we have used the typewriter or word-processing equipment for development, user, operations, and other system documentation. One of the disadvantages of using these media for documentation is that access is limited to those on a distribution list. Documentation in a data dictionary is available to anyone who has access to a computer terminal. Paper is certainly more fragile than the magnetic medium of a dictionary. Documentation in a data dictionary is "living," perpetual documentation; documentation on paper has a limited life span. Although it is possible to perform automated searches on word processing equipment, such searches are often limited to a single document. The automated search and cross-referencing tools of a data dictionary can span multiple programs, systems, databases, report definitions, form definitions, and other categories of documentation.

Historically, system documentation has tended to be inadequate for the following reasons:

1. Little (if any) time is allocated to documentation during the development of a project. Documentation is usually developed after a system is implemented. A whirlwind effort is undertaken to document a system before the designers forget how it works. At this point, there is little incentive to do a good job, since many of the designers will soon be working on other projects or on later stages of the same project. Also, doing all of the documentation at once only increases the unpleasantness of the task.

2. The documentation often does not accurately reflect how the system really works. Because the documentation is usually developed after a system is implemented, it is frequently incomplete and inaccurate. Even if proper documentation controls and management are put in place, there is no way to guarantee that the documentation will agree with the system design.

The programmers and analysts responsible for maintaining a system therefore have little confidence in the reliability of the system documentation. This lack of confidence tends to further reduce the motivation to keep documentation up-to-date. The data dictionary can greatly improve the reliability of documentation about the data used in a system.

The data dictionary itself contains the documentation about the data definitions. By using the dictionary to generate the source program data definitions, the data portion of the program is actually derived from the documentation. This direct link between documentation and system definition guarantees the accuracy of the data documentation. After a system is implemented, all data changes should first be made in the dictionary. Then the source code data changes can be generated from the data dictionary. This assures that the data documentation will be kept up-to-date, and the data processing staff will certainly have more confidence in its accuracy.

Software Generation from a Data Dictionary

A major benefit of the data dictionary is its ability to generate data definitions for a variety of software languages. Dictionaries can generate file and record layouts for use in application languages such as COBOL and PL/1. Data dictionaries can also provide data definitions for procedureless query or report languages such as MARK IV, CULPRIT, NOMAD, and FOCUS.

Dictionaries can also automatically provide data definitions for several database management systems such as IMS, TOTAL, ADABAS, and IDMS. In fact, several major software vendors have bundled their dictionary and DBMS products. By doing so, the DBMS schema and subschema definitions can only be produced from the dictionary.

Recently, commercial data dictionary vendors have enhanced dictionaries to also generate procedure-type source code. For example, these dictionaries could generate COBOL Procedure Division source code from macroinstruction statements contained in the dictionary. MSP's (Manager Software Products, Inc.) Source Manager is an example of this new capability. There are several advantages to generating software from a dictionary.

1. It relieves the application developers of the mundane, repetitive chore of defining and coding data definitions. Likewise, it relieves the database administrator of much of the detail work involved in the data definition language.
2. The dictionary is the source of all entities and attributes. Because all data definitions are automatically derived from the same source, we greatly reduce the inconsistencies and errors that result from manually prepared data descriptions.
3. Because the dictionary is the source of all data definitions, we can more carefully control changes that affect multiple data structures. If a change is made in a particular data element, the dictionary will tell us every place this data element is used. For example, if there is a change in a data element that is used in 10 different data structures, the dictionary provides automated tools to help assure that all 10 data structures will be updated correctly. Without the dictionary, we would have to manually determine where a data element is used. We

would then have to make changes separately in each of the 10 data structures.

4. Some dictionaries provide an audit trail of all changes made in data definitions. This audit trail includes the date and the initiator of these changes.
5. By centralizing the control and generation of data definitions, changes can be made only with the knowledge and consent of data administration. Before a particular data definition is changed, all users of this data definition can be notified of the impending change. Thus, all changes can be made in a controlled, scheduled manner.

Metadata Generation Tools

With some dictionaries, it is possible to produce data definitions that are a combination of both data format and metadata. Figure 2-9 is an example of a COBOL data definition that includes metadata about the data elements contained within the data definition. It is an example of a data definition that could be generated from MSP's Data Manager data dictionary. As it illustrates, metadata is extracted from the dictionary and inserted as comments into the COBOL data definition.

Other metadata generation tools include utilities to generate record/segment layouts from data definitions. Following is a description of a metadata generator from Data Administration, Inc.

The input to this utility could be:

- A data definition contained within the data dictionary

```
 01  EMPLOYEE-INFORMATION.
     05  EMP-SOC-SEC-NBR                      PIC 9(09).
*   A NUMBER ASSIGNED BY THE FEDERAL GOVERNMENT THAT UNIQUELY
*   IDENTIFIES A RESIDENT OF THE COUNTRY
     05  COMPANY-CODE                         PIC X(02).
*   IDENTIFIES THE COMPANY WITHIN THE PARENT CORPORATION
     05  EMP-NAME                             PIC X(30).
*   THE LAST NAME, MIDDLE INITIAL, AND FIRST NAME OF THE EMPLOYEE
     05  EMP-CITY-NAME                        PIC X(20).
*   THE NAME OF THE CITY OR TOWN WHERE THE EMPLOYEE RESIDES
     05  EMP-STATE-CODE                       PIC X(02).
*   THE U.S. POSTAL SERVICE STANDARD ABBREVIATION FOR THE STATE
*   WHERE THE EMPLOYEE LIVES
     05  EMP-CLASSIFICATION-CODE              PIC X(01).
*   A CODE USED TO DESIGNATE HOW THE EMPLOYEE IS PAID
*   H=HOURLY
*   S=SALARY
     05  DATE-LAST-RAISE                      PIC X(06).
*   THE MONTH, DAY, AND YEAR WHEN EMPLOYEE LAST RECEIVED A
*   SALARY OR HOURLY INCREASE
```

Fig. 2-9 Data definition with comments generated by MSP's Data Manager data dictionary.

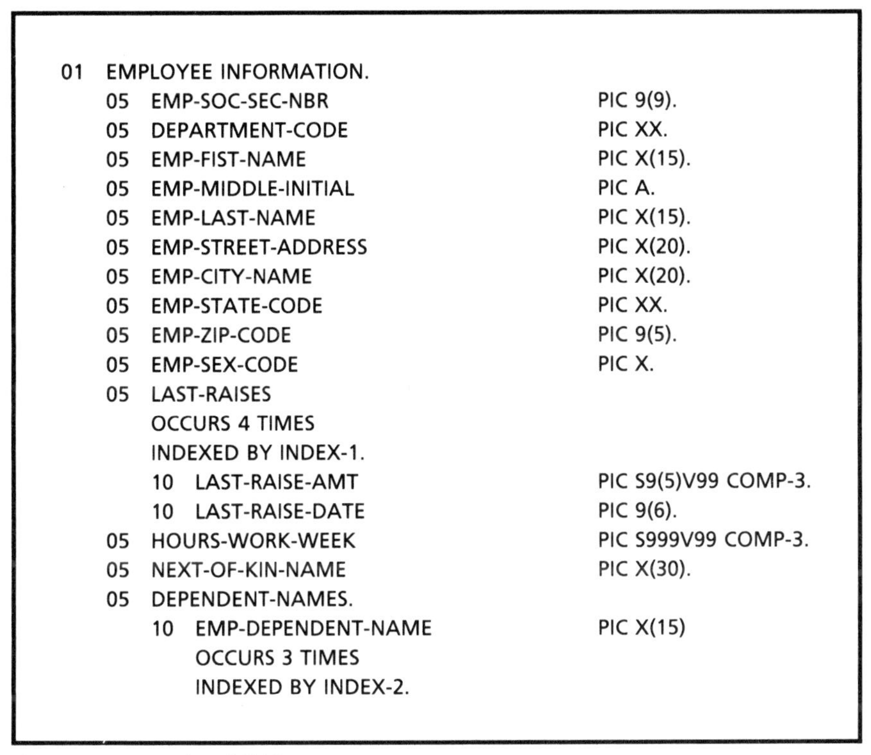

```
01  EMPLOYEE INFORMATION.
    05  EMP-SOC-SEC-NBR                     PIC 9(9).
    05  DEPARTMENT-CODE                     PIC XX.
    05  EMP-FIST-NAME                       PIC X(15).
    05  EMP-MIDDLE-INITIAL                  PIC A.
    05  EMP-LAST-NAME                       PIC X(15).
    05  EMP-STREET-ADDRESS                  PIC X(20).
    05  EMP-CITY-NAME                       PIC X(20).
    05  EMP-STATE-CODE                      PIC XX.
    05  EMP-ZIP-CODE                        PIC 9(5).
    05  EMP-SEX-CODE                        PIC X.
    05  LAST-RAISES
        OCCURS 4 TIMES
        INDEXED BY INDEX-1.
        10  LAST-RAISE-AMT                  PIC S9(5)V99 COMP-3.
        10  LAST-RAISE-DATE                 PIC 9(6).
    05  HOURS-WORK-WEEK                     PIC S999V99 COMP-3.
    05  NEXT-OF-KIN-NAME                    PIC X(30).
    05  DEPENDENT-NAMES.
        10  EMP-DEPENDENT-NAME              PIC X(15)
            OCCURS 3 TIMES
            INDEXED BY INDEX-2.
```

Fig. 2-10 COBOL data definition.

- Entire source code libraries (PANVALET, LIBRARIAN, COPYLIB, etc.)
- Individual programs
- Individual record or segment definitions

Figure 2-10 is a sample COBOL record definition that could be input to this utility.

Figure 2-11 is a sample printout of a "vertical" record layout of the COBOL data definition from Figure 2-10. This utility automatically calculates the beginning position, ending position, and length of all data elements.

Figure 2-12 is an example of a "horizontal" record layout generated from the COBOL source code in Figure 2-10. This utility provides data users with a graphic display, or "picture," of data definitions. This report is useful in portraying the spatial relationship or size of one data element as compared with other data elements.

The automated record layout generators described above have two

DATADRAW VERTICAL RECORD LAYOUT DATE = 05/11/82 PAGE 1

RECORD-NAME = EMPLOYEE-INFORMATION DATA ADMINISTRATION INC, USE BY AGREEMENT ONLY

DATA ELEM. NO.	LEVEL	DATA NAME	POSITION FROM	POSITION TO	LENGTH	FORMAT	PICTURE	REDE-FINES	OCCURS
1	01	EMPLOYEE-INFORMATION	1	208	208	GROUP			
2	05	EMP-SOC-SEC-NBR	1	9	9	NUMERIC	9(9)		
3	05	DEPARTMENT-CODE	10	11	2	ALPHANUMERIC	XX		
4	05	EMP-FIRST-NAME	12	26	15	ALPHANUMERIC	X(15)		
5	05	EMP-MIDDLE-INITIAL	27	27	1	ALPHABETIC	A		
6	05	EMP-LAST-NAME	28	42	15	ALPHANUMERIC	X(15)		
7	05	EMP-STREET-ADDRESS	43	62	20	ALPHANUMERIC	X(20)		
8	05	EMP-CITY-NAME	63	82	20	ALPHANUMERIC	X(20)		
9	05	EMP-STATE-CODE	83	84	2	ALPHANUMERIC	XX		
10	05	EMP-ZIP-CODE	85	89	5	NUMERIC	9(5)		
11	05	EMP-SEX-CODE	90	90	1	ALPHANUMERIC	X		
12	05	LAST-RAISES	91	130	40	GROUP			4
13	10	LAST-RAISE-AMT	91	94	4	PACKED DECIMAL	S9(5)V99		
14	10	LAST-RAISE-DATE	95	100	6	NUMERIC	9(6)		
15	10	LAST-RAISE-AMT	101	104	4	PACKED DECIMAL	S9(5)V99		
16	10	LAST-RAISE-DATE	105	110	6	NUMERIC	9(6)		
17	10	LAST-RAISE-AMT	111	114	4	PACKED DECIMAL	S9(5)V99		
18	10	LAST-RAISE-DATE	115	120	6	NUMERIC	9(6)		
19	10	LAST-RAISE-AMT	121	124	4	PACKED DECIMAL	S9(5)V99		
20	10	LAST-RAISE-DATE	125	130	6	NUMERIC	9(6)		
21	05	HOURS-WORK-WEEK	131	133	3	PACKED DECIMAL	S999V99		
22	05	NEXT-OF-KIN-NAME	134	163	30	ALPHANUMERIC	X(30)		
23	05	DEPENDENT-NAMES	164	208	45	GROUP			3
24	10	EMP-DEPENDENT-NAME	164	178	15	ALPHANUMERIC	X(15)		

Fig. 2-11 Vertical record layout of COBOL data definition.

```
                                   DATADRAW HORIZONTAL RECORD LAYOUT            DATE = 05/11/82       PAGE   1
                                                                 DATA ADMINISTRATION INC, USE BY AGREEMENT ONLY
RECORD NAME = EMPLOYEE-INFORMATION
*
|---------|--|---------------|-|---------------|--------------------|--------------------|--|-----|-|----|------|----------|
|EMP      |D |EMP FIRST NAME |E|EMP LAST NAME  |EMP STREET ADDRESS  |EMP CITY NAME       |E |EMP  |E|L   |LAST  |OCCURS 002|
|SOC      |E |               |M|               |                    |                    |M |ZIP  |M|A   |RAISE |          |
|SEC      |P |               |P|               |                    |                    |P |CODE |P|S   |DATE  |          |
|NBR      |A |               | |               |                    |                    |  |     | |T   |      |          |
|         |R |               |M|               |                    |                    |S |     |S|    |      |          |
|         |T |               |I|               |                    |                    |T |     |E|R   |      |          |
|         |M |               |D|               |                    |                    |A |     |X|A   |      |          |
|         |E |               |D|               |                    |                    |T |     | |I   |      |          |
|         |N |               |L|               |                    |                    |E |     |C|S   |      |          |
|         |T |               |E|               |                    |                    |  |     |O|E   |      |          |
|         |  |               | |               |                    |                    |C |     |D|    |      |          |
|         |C |               |I|               |                    |                    |O |     |E|A   |      |          |
|         |O |               |N|               |                    |                    |D |     | |M   |      |          |
|         |D |               |I|               |                    |                    |E |     | |T   |      |          |
|         |E |               |T|               |                    |                    |  |     | |    |      |          |
|         |  |               |I|               |                    |                    |  |     | |    |      |          |
|---------|--|---------------|-|---------------|--------------------|--------------------|--|-----|-|----|------|----------|
|999999999|XX|XXXXXXXXXXXXXXX|A|XXXXXXXXXXXXXXX|XXXXXXXXXXXXXXXXXXXX|XXXXXXXXXXXXXXXXXXXX|XX|99999|X|PPPP|999999|0000000000|
|         |  |               | |               |                    |                    |  |     | |S . |      |          |
|---------|--|---------------|-|---------------|--------------------|--------------------|--|-----|-|----|------|----------|

                                                                                                        1          1
          1 1             2 2             4                    6                    8  8     9 9    9      0          1
1         0 2             7 8             3                    3                    3  5     0 1    5      1          0

|----------|----------|---|--------------------|---------------|---------------|---------------|
|OCCURS 003|OCCURS 004|H  |NEXT OF KIN NAME    |EMP            |OCCURS 002     |OCCURS 003     |
|          |          |O  |                    |DEPENDENT      |               |               |
|          |          |U  |                    |NAME           |               |               |
|          |          |R  |                    |               |               |               |
|          |          |S  |                    |               |               |               |
|          |          |   |                    |               |               |               |
|          |          |W  |                    |               |               |               |
|          |          |O  |                    |               |               |               |
|          |          |R  |                    |               |               |               |
|          |          |K  |                    |               |               |               |
|          |          |   |                    |               |               |               |
|          |          |W  |                    |               |               |               |
|          |          |E  |                    |               |               |               |
|          |          |E  |                    |               |               |               |
|          |          |K  |                    |               |               |               |
|          |          |   |                    |               |               |               |
|----------|----------|---|--------------------|---------------|---------------|---------------|
|0000000000|0000000000|PPP|XXXXXXXXXXXXXXXXXXXX|XXXXXXXXXXXXXXX|000000000000000|000000000000000|
|          |          |S. |                    |               |               |               |
|----------|----------|---|--------------------|---------------|---------------|---------------|

1          1          1  1                    1               1               1              2
1          2          3  3                    6               7               9              0
1          1          1  4                    4               9               4              8
```

Fig. 2-12 Horizontal record layout of COBOL data definition.

advantages over manually drawn record layouts. First, they eliminate the time and cost expended by data processing staff members in producing hand-drawn layouts. Second, they assure that data definition documentation accurately reflects the contents of source code libraries. Each time a change is made in a data definition in the data dictionary or source code library, this utility can produce an up-to-date layout for that data definition. In this way, the data documentation and the dictionary will always be consistent.

Utilizing the End-User Resource

The data processing industry has recently undergone a healthy reform. Techniques in both hardware and software have been developed to utilize the end-user staff in assisting data processing employees in the development of automated systems.

Minicomputers, microcomputers, fourth-generation languages, and user-friendly inquiry and reporting tools are means by which we can utilize the user in the development of data processing systems. The data dictionary is one more tool to increase user involvement in system development. Figure 2-13 illustrates the user-data processing staff involvement in the traditional system development life cycle.

While we have made significant gains in user interaction and review during the different phases of system development, this process still relies too heavily on the very limited data processing resource. In this traditional development scheme, the user is still only a reviewer and auditor of our system development efforts. The user really does not actively participate in the analysis and design effort itself.

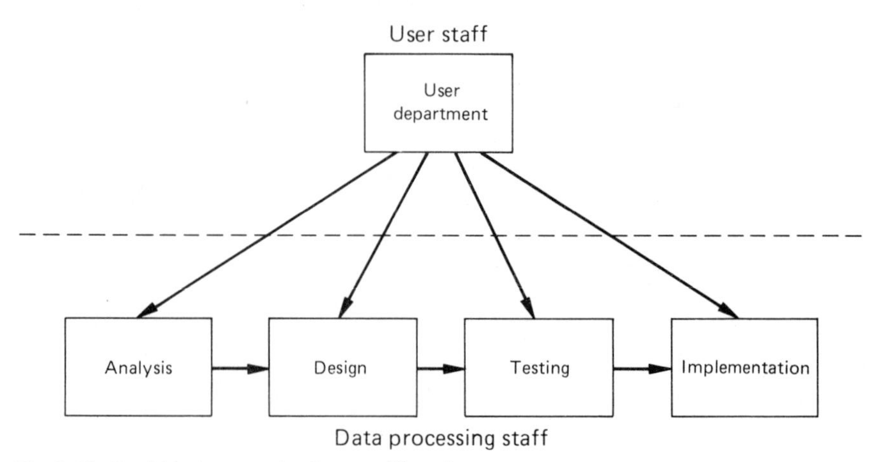

Fig. 2-13 Traditional system development life cycle.

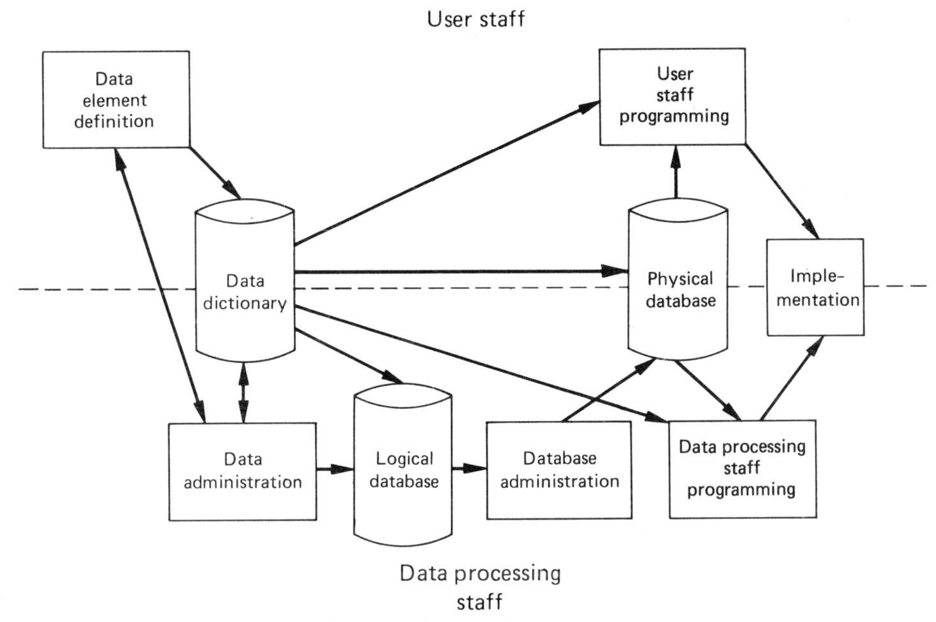

Fig. 2-14 System development life cycle using data dictionary.

The data dictionary, when used with other modern development aids, can help balance the DP-user staff workload. Figure 2-14 illustrates a system development process using the data dictionary. This development process would work as follows:

1. With the assistance of the data administration staff, the user defines the data elements used to perform day-to-day business functions. These data elements are collected from all of the input forms and reports used in the end user's daily operations. These data elements would, in fact, comprise the majority of all the data processing system data elements. The only other data elements needed would be those necessary to define the system and program controls. These data elements would later be defined by the data processing staff during the design phase.
2. Using the data characteristics and relationships defined on the data dictionary, a logical database model is created.
3. Using the logical database model, and knowledge of the physical constraints of the hardware, database manager, and operating system, the database administration staff builds a physical database.
4. Depending upon the complexity of the process, and the interface of this process with existing systems, each process is coded by either the

user or data processing staff. The coding process may use traditional languages or user-friendly procedureless languages.

The data dictionary is a tool to more effectively utilize the talents of both user and data processing personnel. By defining the characteristics, relationships, and editing criteria of the data, the user can be directly involved in the design of the system. The user will have more direct control over system design and, at the same time, save data processing staff time in the definition of data. The data dictionary is a tool to delegate more of the data processing workload and responsibility to the user community.

Chapter 3

STANDARDS, POLICIES, AND PROCEDURES FOR DATA USE

This chapter contains a comprehensive discussion of data administration standards. But before discussing the details of DA standards, it is important that data administrators understand the general philosophy and implications of these standards. The section entitled "A Word of Warning about DA Standards" will help prepare data administrators for the realities of the data processing world. Before introducing DA standards to an organization, the non-DA staff must first be introduced to the general concept and terminology of data administration. This chapter also contains an introduction to DA terminology.

THE TEN COMMANDMENTS OF DA STANDARDS

1. The first rule is that there are exceptions to every rule. No standard is applicable in every situation. However, the DA staff must not allow exceptions to become the norm.
2. Management must support and be willing to help enforce standards. If standards are violated, management must assist in assuring that the violations are corrected.
3. Standards must be practical, viable, and workable. Standards must be based upon common sense. The less complicated and cumbersome the standards, the more they will be adhered to. *Keep standards simple.*
4. Standards must not be absolute; there must be some room for flexibility. While some standards must be strictly adhered to, most standards should not be so rigid that they severely restrict the freedom of the data designer.

5. Standards should not be retroactive. Standards are to control and manage present and future actions—not to undo and redo past actions. In most cases, standards enacted today cannot apply to data design that began several months ago.
6. Standards must be easily enforceable. To achieve this, it must be easy to detect violations in standards. The more the process of auditing for the compliance of standards can be automated, the more effective will be the standards themselves. (See Automated Tools to Assist in Enforcing DA Naming Conventions, later in this chapter, for a discussion of automated tools to help enforce DA standards.)
7. Standards must be sold, not dictated. Even if upper management wholeheartedly supports DA standards, the standards must be sold to employees at all levels. DA must be willing to advertise the standards to all employees and to justify the need for such standards. DA standards demand that programmers and analysts change the way they design data. Any lasting and meaningful change must come from the employees themselves.
8. The details about the standards themselves are not important—the important thing is to *have* some standards. DA must be willing to compromise and negotiate the details of the standards to be enacted.
9. Standards should be enacted gradually. Do not attempt to put all DA standards in place at the same time. Once standards are enacted, begin to enforce them, but do it gradually and tactfully. Allow ample time for the non-DA staff to react and adjust to new standards. The implementation of standards must be an evolutionary, rather than a revolutionary, process.
10. The most important standard in data administration is the standard of consistency—consistency of data naming, data attributes, data design, and data use.

Before an organization implements any DA standards, it is important that a data administrator be able to communicate effectively with non-data administration personnel. To do this, non-DA personnel must be introduced to some basic data administration–data dictionary terminology. Data Administration Fundamentals, below, provides a detailed explanation for the most commonly used DA terms. Appendix A contains a complete glossary of DA terminology.

A WORD OF WARNING ABOUT DA STANDARDS

Introducing and implementing DA standards within an organization can be a difficult, and prolonged undertaking. DA standards require changes in the way data processors perform their jobs. These changes involve the design and use of data. DA standards require consistency and discipline of data use where none formerly existed.

Data processors tend to be imaginative, creative people. In general, they do not enjoy doing the same things the same way over and over again. Yet we must persuade them to always refer to the same entity by the same data name. We must persuade them to always use the same characteristics or formats for like entities. We must convince them of the benefits of data consistency.

Data processors also tend to be introverted and independent workers. They are not always receptive to the idea of using data that was designed by someone else (either by data administration or by another analyst). Data processors also resist the use of packaged data for the same reason they resist proprietary software—because it was "not invented here."

With the introduction of DA standards, many data processors must begin to justify their design and use of the data resource. After coding a program, the average programmer can justify the design and structure of that program. However, many programmers cannot explain how they designed and structured data elements within a record, segment, or table. Most programmers cannot rationalize their data designs in terms of modularity or reduction in future maintenance costs. For the first time in their careers, they must justify data design to data administration. This is a difficult transition for many data processors. This restriction or loss of freedom in data design is seen as an inconvenience and nuisance to many.

The data administrator must attempt to introduce *data* concepts into a data processing world that is *systems* oriented. Data processors traditionally think in terms of processes, procedures, and systems—not in terms of data. DA must try to complement this tradition by exposing data processors to the *data* aspect of *data* processing.

Data processing management and the end user are often more receptive to data administration standards than are the DP applications development and maintenance staff. The database administration staff will normally welcome DA standards before the application developers will. The standardization of data is also consistent with the goals of quality assurance and internal audit. It is often advantageous to first gain support from these areas before approaching the application development staff.

Before attempting to implement DA standards, the following questions should be answered:

1. Which managers, in which sequence, should be approached for support in implementing DA standards?
2. Which managers understand the role of DA within the organization?

3. Are there any managers who formerly worked in companies that had a DA organization?
4. Does your organization now have a quality assurance or quality control section?
5. Who is the most and who is the least receptive to change?

Because data processors have been raised in a world of data incompatibility and inconsistency, they commonly are suspicious and skeptical about the quality of data created by others. For the same reasons, once data processors create and gain control over their own data, they are somewhat reluctant to allow others to share this data. The "pride of ownership" of data presents a real challenge to the data administrator. It is the job of data administration to deregulate and socialize the ownership of data.

WHY DO WE NEED DATA ADMINISTRATION STANDARDS?

Improve the Quality of Documentation

DA standards require meaningful, descriptive definitions for all data elements. Without sufficient data documentation, data processing systems have traditionally been plagued with data redundancies and inconsistencies. This also contributes to errors of data incompatibility during the development and operation of data processing systems.

Naming standards make an entity name more meaningful and self-documenting. With a meaningful name for the entity, the name itself portrays information to the user of an entity. For those users of a data entity who are unable or unwilling to reference additional information about a data entity, the entity name itself is the first source of information about its purpose and content.

Although COBOL has been touted as a "self-documenting" language, COBOL naming standards are necessary to help document the data usage in this language. DA standards require meaningful, unique data element names. These standards provide better documentation than the traditional nondescriptive data names assigned by programmers.

DA standards concerning the identification, classification, and nomenclature of data are important: they enable us to write and speak the same "data" language. We define and document data in a variety of media throughout an organization. Below are examples of some of the media of data documentation.

- Corporate policy and practices
- Program source code

- Data flow diagrams
- Flowcharts
- Structure charts
- Pseudocode
- Decision tables
- Functional specifications

With data administration standards, it is possible to improve the consistency of data references throughout these documentation media.

Enforce Consistency of Data Use

With rigorous and comprehensive naming standards, it is easier to detect and reduce the occurrence of homonyms, synonyms, and aliases of data entities. By doing so, we can minimize redundant or duplicate entities used in our data processing systems. This not only reduces the total number of data elements used in a system, but minimizes further maintenance to duplicate data fields.

As we will see later in the section Data Attributes, DA attribute standards help to minimize the need for different versions or variations of data entities. This reduces the need for data transformations that are so common in the data processing systems of yesteryear.

Improve the Accuracy and Efficiency of Data Use

DA standards improve the way we identify and classify data entities used throughout an organization. By providing consistent and meaningful names for data elements, we improve the accuracy of searches for a particular piece of data. It is also easier to associate and retrieve elements that have similar characteristics or uses.

DA standards also minimize the possibility of inconsistencies and irregularities when updating or retrieving data from a complex database. Normalization standards (discussed later in this chapter) provide rules and procedures to safeguard our systems from anomalies that may occur during the maintenance of a database.

Reduce the Size and Complexity of Data Processing Systems

Many of the DA standards discussed within this chapter are designed to increase our efficient and proficient use of the data resource. Traditionally, we have been inept in our use of data. Let's consider the different ways that we use data. Basically, we act upon data in two ways—we compute data or we transform data. The following lists contain examples of these two uses of data. The uses are categorized by the verbs used to describe the actions applied to data.

Computations	Transformations		
ADD	MOVE	EXPAND	EXTRACT
SUBTRACT	SHIFT	IMPLODE	LEFT-JUSTIFY
MULTIPLY	COPY	EXPLODE	RIGHT-JUSTIFY
DIVIDE	INVERT	CONDENSE	ZERO-FILL
IF	REVERSE	CONTRACT	PAD
	CONVERT	COMPRESS	TRUNCATE
	SPLIT	COMPARE	MASK
	MERGE	PACK	SUPPRESS
	CONSOLIDATE	UNPACK	INHIBIT
	COMPACT	REFORMAT	

The majority of the lines of code in a system are not devoted to computations with data, but are consumed in the transformation of data. Because of inefficient and inconsistent use of data, we have forced ourselves to become masters of the contortion and distortion of data. We waste an enormous amount of our system resources in the transformations of data because we have not applied rigorous standards for the proficient use of data. How many programs have been designed and implemented to achieve nothing but the conversion of data from one format to another?

By minimizing the number of data transformations, the auditing and accounting necessary to verify the conversions is also reduced. In other words, when data is converted from one form to another, auditing trails are necessary to assure us that the data was converted accurately. The following are examples of some of the auditing consequences of data transformations. They represent auditing processes and entities required as a result of data transformations.

BALANCING
CONTROL TOTALS
CROSS-FOOTING
HEADER RECORDS
TRAILER RECORDS
HASH TOTALS
CHECK DIGITS

Techniques to minimize data transformations will be discussed throughout this chapter.

Increase the Modularity and Flexibility of a System

By applying normalization and other DA standards, we can minimize redundancy, overlap, and coupling between data elements. By thus compartmentalizing our data structures, we isolate the data elements that might be affected by a future change in data processing requirements. This reduces the number of data elements that would have to be changed, thereby reducing the cost of future maintenance of the data structures used in our systems.

DATA ADMINISTRATION FUNDAMENTALS

Since COBOL is by far the most commonly used programming language, most of the illustrations and examples used in this chapter are in reference to the COBOL language. All examples of data element naming standards are in reference to COBOL data names. However, because of the severe restrictions imposed by some languages (e.g., BAL or BASIC) on the length of the data name, it is not possible to apply these naming standards to the language alias name. However, regardless of the programming language used, the naming conventions in this chapter can, and should, be applied to the primary, or end-user, name for a data element. Many of the DA standards discussed in this chapter can be applied to any data design, regardless of the hardware or software on which the data design is implemented.

Fundamental Data Administration Definitions

Data element The smallest unit of information in a data dictionary. The smallest unit of information that can be perceived or understood by an end user.

Example: EMPLOYEE-FIRST-NAME
SOCIAL-SECURITY-NUMBER

Group A combination of data elements and/or other groups.

Example:	Date:	group of *year, month,* and *day*
	Record or segment:	group of data elements
	File:	group of records
	Database:	group of segments

Attributes The physical characteristics or properties of a data element. An attribute helps define and describe a piece of data.

Example: Length
Format
Definition
Editing characteristics (valid values)

The attributes of a data element are analogous to the attributes of a human being:

Height
Weight
Hair color
Eye color

Synonym A different name or identifier for the same entity.

Example: EMPLOYEE-NUMBER and PAYROLL-NUMBER
EMPLOYMENT-DATE and START-DATE

In general, a data element is a synonym of some other element if the two elements have the same definition.

Example: EMPLOYEE-NUMBER and PAYROLL-NUMBER are synonyms if they both have the following definition:

The unique identifier of an employee within a company.

Example: CAR and AUTOMOBILE are synonyms.

Homonym Two or more data elements are homonyms if they have the same name (e.g., COBOL data name) but have different meanings.

Example: ACCOUNT-NUMBER in the accounts payable system could be a homonym of ACCOUNT-NUMBER in the accounts receivable system.

Example: TRAIN (as in railroad) is a homonym of TRAIN (to teach).

Alias A different way of referring to the same entity. Usually refers to different programming language names for the same thing. An alias is a data processing synonym.

Example: Generic name: EMPLOYEE-SOCIAL-SECURITY-NUMBER
COBOL alias: EMP-SOC-SEC-NBR
FOCUS alias: EMPNUMBER
IMS alias: EMPNBR

Version A different variation of the same entity. Something that has the same value but has a different attribute.

Example: SOCIAL-SECURITY-NUMBER

Version 1 PIC 9(9)
Version 2 PIC S9(9) COMP-3
Version 3 PIC X(9)

Acronym A word formed from the first letter of several words

Example: COD *C*ash *o*n *d*elivery
TIP *T*o *i*nsure *p*romptness
ZIP *Z*one *i*mprovement *p*lan

Abbreviation A shortening of a word or words

Example:

Word	*Abbreviation*
ACCOUNT	ACCT
CORPORATION	CORP
NUMBER	NBR

The Structure of a Data Element

- Ours is the business of data management.
- We cannot manage that which we cannot identify.
- We cannot identify that which we cannot accurately name.

A building is only as good as its foundation. The quality of the data element is the key to the sound foundation for all data structures. Unless proper consideration is given to the creation and naming of data elements, the quality of the entire data structure will be sacrificed. In the following sections, we will discuss several considerations important to the quality of the data element.

Regardless of the language used, the design of data elements should be based upon logical (rather than physical) characteristics. Data elements should be assigned logical (rather than physical) names. We should create and name data elements according to the purpose or function of this data element, not according to how, where, and when the data element is used. Data elements should have logical, not physical, constructs.

Logical	*Physical*
What	Where
	When
	How
	Who

However, data entities have traditionally been created according to how and where they are used, rather than according to what they really are. For example, in a data processing system, data entity names are often associated with the physical files or the programs that use them.

The data element XB-FILE-STATUS-CODE is an example. When creating data elements, we should remove the physical data processing characteristics from the element itself.

If we design a data element according to where it is used (e.g., a STATUS-CODE in the XB-FILE), we severely restrict the flexibility of the entity. For example, suppose the XA and the XB files are redesigned into one file. To accommodate this, must all of the data element names which begin with XA- and XB- be changed to XA-XB-? By creating and naming data elements generically, the data element itself is independent of the physical location of its use or the application itself.

By disassociating a data element from physical data processing characteristics, it becomes a more modular and flexible data entity. This minimizes the need for aliases or redundancy if it is used elsewhere. Data elements should be designed and named so that they can span multiple applications and organizations. Instead of creating the data elements XA-FILE-STATUS-CODE and XB-FILE-STATUS-CODE, we should create the data elements FILE-ID and FILE-STATUS-CODE. Thus, FILE-ID and FILE-STATUS-CODE can be used anywhere in a data processing system, for a variety of files, and still retain their basic meaning and purpose. This eliminates the need to create aliases that depend upon where or how the data element is used.

Even the simplest entity often has multiple meanings and definitions within a large organization. A term as simple as POLICY-NUMBER is perceived as many different things to different employees in an insurance company. The term ACCOUNT-NUMBER also has multiple meanings depending upon where it is used. When naming a data element, you should consider how others in your organization might view that data element. How does ACCOUNT-NUMBER differ from PAY-VENDOR-ACCT-NBR or GENERAL-LEDGER-ACCT-NBR? How does STATUS-CODE differ from EMP-DEDUCTION-STATUS-CODE or CONTRACT-PO-STATUS-CODE?

When developing a system or data structure, it is essential to eliminate confusion over the names and definitions of several similar data entities. When confusion or conflict exists, meetings should be held to resolve definitions of data elements. It is important to involve as many different user groups as possible in such discussions.

The amount of detail to be included in a data name is directly proportionate to the scope of the data dictionary where the entity is to be stored. Does the assigned name easily distinguish this data element name from all other entities in the dictionary? Will the data elements in this logical/physical dictionary later migrate to a larger corporate dictionary? Can this data element be easily distinguished from the data elements in the corporate dictionary?

The dictionary name assigned to a data element should be derived from the definition of the data element itself. The dictionary name of an element should reflect the purpose of the entity, not how the element is perceived or used by any one group within the enterprise. Assigning a data name according to its use within one user department may have little or no relevance to other users. For example, do not create two different entities for PAYROLL-EMP-SOC-SEC-NBR and PERSONNEL-EMP-SOC-SEC-NBR, but create instead one generic data element: EMP-SOC-SEC-NBR.

In summary, a data element should be designed:

1. According to logical, not physical, characteristics
2. Independent of the hardware or software where it is used
3. Independent of any particular user organization

A data element name should be:

1. As meaningful as possible
2. Self-documenting
3. Easily distinguishable from other data elements in a dictionary
4. Derived from the definition of the entity
5. A general or generic name

Data Element Naming Standards

Every data element should be composed of:

1. One class word
2. One prime word
3. One or more modifying words

Example: ACCOUNTS-PAY-VENDOR-NUMBER

Class word ⟶ NUMBER
Prime word ⟶ VENDOR
Modifier word ⟶ ACCOUNTS
Modifier word ⟶ PAY

A class word is the most important noun in a data element name.

Example: **Class words**

Code	STATE-TAX-CODE
Date	EMPLOYEE-HIRE-DATE
Hours	EMPL-OVERTIME-HOURS-WORKED
Percent	FEDERAL-INCOME-TAX-PERCENT

Class words are used to identify and describe the general purpose (or use) of a data element. This allows us to categorize and search for data elements based upon their use in data processing systems. Below is a list of the most frequently used class words:

AMOUNT	NAME
CODE	NUMBER
CONSTANT	PERCENT
COUNT	TEXT
DATE	TIME

See the section entitled Standard Abbreviations and Acronyms for a list of IBM-recognized class words.

A prime word is the most important modifier of the class word. It describes the object being defined.

Example: **Prime Words**

TAX	STATE-TAX-CODE
EMPLOYEE	EMPLOYEE-HIRE-DATE
ACCOUNT	GENERAL-LEDGER-ACCOUNT-NUMBER

Prime words are entity classes or subgroups of entity classes of an organization.

Example: **Entity Classes**

ACCOUNTING	FACILITY	PLANNING
BUDGET	INVENTORY	PROCUREMENT
CUSTOMER	MANUFACTURING	PRODUCT
DISTRIBUTION	MARKETING	RESEARCH
EMPLOYEE	ORDERS	SALES
ENGINEERING	PAYMENTS	SUPPLIER

Example: Prime words in the EMPLOYEE entity class:

SPOUSE
DEPENDENT
WAGES
DEDUCTIONS

Some DA installations require a prime word or a class word to be the first or last word in a data name. These standards usually were created to facilitate the manual scanning of new data names to verify that they contained class and prime words. However, with modern automated search techniques, this standard is no longer necessary. (See Automated Tools to Assist in Enforcing DA Naming Conventions, below.)

A name should be assigned as it would be used in normal speech. This makes the data name more "user friendly." The arrangement or sequencing of the words within a name is not important.

Example: Do not name ⟶ EMPLOYEE-ADDRESS-STREET
Name instead ⟶ EMPLOYEE-STREET-ADDRESS

Further Considerations for Constructing Data Elements

In this section we will discuss the implications of achieving well-structured data elements and alternative ways to meet this objective. The ultimate objective of data processing is to provide information cheaply and accurately to a variety of users. These users should not need the knowledge or the assistance of data processing personnel. The information customer should be able to use a computer to answer questions expressed in the language of the customer, and not the language of the data processing professional. For example, the vice president of a company should be able to type (or better yet, to dictate) to a computer a question such as:

WHAT WERE THE TOTAL FIRST QUARTER ADVERTISING EXPENSES FOR THE SOUTH-EASTERN DIVISION, SUMMARIZED BY PRODUCT?

It is hoped that we should be able to provide the consumer with an information commodity as easily as we would supply other commodities. The consumer need not understand how this commodity is procured. Ultimately, we should strive to provide the masses with information "vending machines" (see Figure 3-1).

There are several disciplines within data processing that are striving to achieve this objective. Some of these disciplines include artificial intelligence, database management systems technology, and query languages. However, the objective of providing accurate and reliable information will be unattainable unless we standardize the data from which this information is extracted.

Unless our databases are constructed from a foundation of clear, concise, and standardized data elements, accurate or reliable assimilation of this data is impossible. Data is of minimal value unless it can be combined/totaled or compared with other data. Unless the component data parts are compatible, synthesis of information from data cannot be performed.

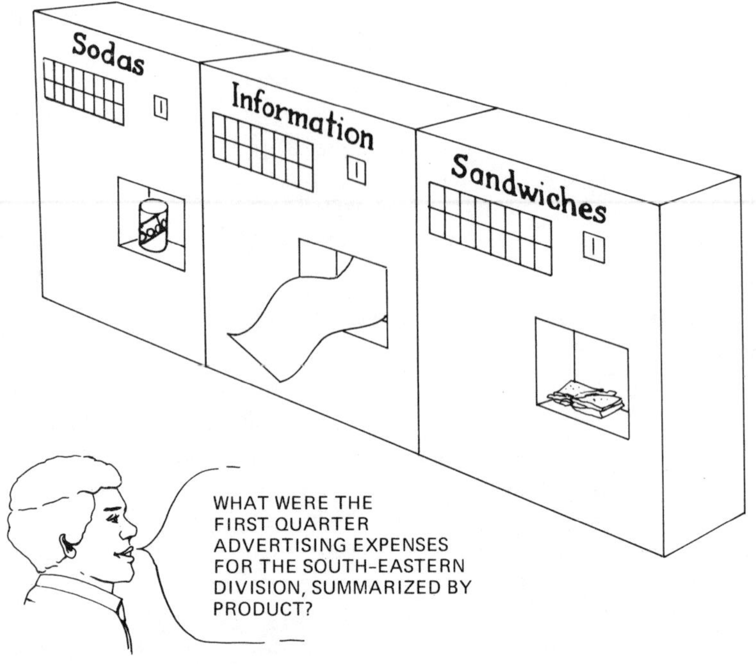

Fig. 3-1 Information vending machine.

The Information "Vending Machine" The following scenario describes the problem of inaccuracy and unreliability of information caused by a lack of data standardization.

Let us assume that the Acme Aerospace Company is under contract to the Air Force to develop a strategic bomber. All phases of the project are on schedule except for the testing of the wing aerodynamics. The construction and testing of the wing assemblies are four weeks behind schedule. To compound this problem, the chief aerodynamics engineer has just submitted his resignation and will be leaving the company in two weeks. The project manager has asked the personnel department to immediately find a replacement.

The data processing department of the Acme Company recently implemented an employee-related information retrieval system for the personnel department. This system uses artificial intelligence to interpret the end-user requests or queries for data. This system also permits access to the 12 different employee-related databases. The personnel department hopes to use this system to search for a qualified candidate to replace the departing aerodynamics engineer.

The personnel manager logs on to a terminal and types in the following request:

GIVE ME THE NAMES OF ALL ENGINEERS WHO HAVE BEEN WITH THE COMPANY FOR AT LEAST FIVE YEARS AND HAVE AT LEAST THREE YEARS OF EXPERIENCE IN AIRCRAFT WING AERODYNAMICS.

There are four databases that contain data which identifies the job classification code for employees. The remaining eight databases contain information that may or may not be useful in identifying engineers. For example, two files only describe employees as *clerical, technical,* or *management.* But it is impossible to determine if engineers are within the *technical* classification. The remaining databases contain a *functional-area code;* however, some *functional areas* contain *engineering, accounting,* and *clerical* job descriptions. Therefore, we can use only the data contained within four databases. This data is interrogated for the different codes that identify engineers.

The next step involves calculating the years of experience with the company for those engineers previously selected. Years of experience is equal to current date minus the date when the employee was hired. However the various employee databases contain conflicting data concerning an employee's hire date. On these files, there are various data names that may or may not define hire date. These data names are as follows:

EMPLOYEE-START-DATE
EMP-EMPLOYMENT-DATE
EMPL-HIRE-DT
EMPLOYEE-BEGIN-DATE
START-DATE-OF-EMPL

Are these fields equivalent? Is EMPL-HIRE-DT the day when the employee was enrolled with the company, and EMPLOYEE-BEGIN-DATE the first day of employment? Can the two dates be different?

There is yet a further complication. Some of the databases contain employee records with precalculated number of years with the company. The names of these fields are:

NBR-YRS-SENIORITY
YEARS-WITH-COMPANY
COMPANY-SEN-YRS

Should we extract the years-of-experience data, or should we calculate this based upon hire date and current date? If we use the years-of-experience data, must we also interrogate the leave-of-absence data? For example, an engineer could have been hired six years ago, but could have taken a three-year leave of absence. Does this engineer qualify for the search argument "... HAVE BEEN WITH THE COMPANY FOR AT LEAST FIVE YEARS . . ."?

As this scenario demonstrates, it is virtually impossible to extract information from data that lacks standards or consistency. This scenario also illustrates the difference between information and data. This difference is analogous to the difference between understanding and facts. For example, many could memorize certain facts about the atomic chart, but few people can apply these facts to the understanding of chemistry and physics. Information is usable data.

Although the Acme Aerospace Company files contained an abundance of employee data, very little reliable information could be extracted from this data. This is typical of most data processing installations and enterprises that are drowning in data yet thirsty for information. Data without standards cannot be assimilated into information.

"Core" Data Elements The current periodic table of elements, the *atomic chart,* lists approximately 100 elements. All matter, as we know it, is composed of these atoms or combinations of these atoms. For example, atoms of hydrogen (H) and oxygen (O) can be combined to form a variety of materials. H_2O, water, and H_2O_2, hydrogen peroxide, are examples of some of the combinations of these simple elements.

It is possible to derive a very large number of entities from different occurrences and combinations of relatively few types of atoms.

Scientists and chemists also have a standard and consistent method of labeling all matter based on the atomic construction of that matter. How does this compare with the way a layman would label matter? For purposes of illustration, let us compare in Table 3-1 how a scientist and a layman could label or identify the same element, water:

Table 3-1

Scientist's label	*Layman's labels*	
H_2O	Water	Snow
	Precipitation	Flurries
	Rain	Sleet
	Drizzle	Hail
	Mist	Fog
	Humidity	Dew
	Haze	Frost
	Moisture	

In addition, water is often labeled according to its temperature variants. For example, in Table 3-2:

Table 3-2

Label	*Temperature variant*
Ice	below 32° F
Water	between 32° F and 212° F
Steam	above 212° F

However, all of these identities or labels of data could be reduced to a relatively few constructs. For example, the two fields ELEMENT-CODE and TEMPERATURE-AMOUNT could suffice to accurately identify the different variants of WATER.

Since all known matter can be derived from a small number of atoms, then all known matter is related in its atomic or chemical composition. Likewise, all data in our data processing systems are related. The only variance is the strengths or weaknesses of these relationships. For example, the relationship between EMPLOYEE-NUMBER and EMPLOYEE-NAME is fairly obvious. What about such apparently disjointed entities as EMPLOYEE-NUMBER and PART-NUMBER? Although EMPLOYEE-NUMBER is contained within the human resource system, and PART-NUMBER occurs almost exclusively within the manufacturing system, they are related. The relationships below illustrate this connection.

- Certain employees (EMPLOYEE-NUMBERS) are assigned to certain ASSEMBLY-LINES
- Each ASSEMBLY-LINE performs a certain number of TASKS
- Each TASK involves the assembly or finishing of certain parts (PART-NUMBERS)

Therefore, certain EMPLOYEES normally work with certain PART-NUMBERS.

As explained earlier, all matter is built on a foundation of a relatively small number of *atomic building blocks*. If all matter can be labeled and constructed from a relatively few constructs of atoms, why is it that data processors cannot construct and label all data based upon a finite number of *"core" data elements?* Why is it that the source code libraries of a typical data processing installation contain hundreds of thousands of data element names? Are these names just variations and permutations (synonyms and aliases) of a relatively few "core" data elements? In other words, are all data molecules formed from a finite number of data atoms?

Let us attempt to approximate the total number of unique entities necessary for communicating within our data processing systems. Let us equate the number of entities used within the English language with the number of entities used within a programming language. The average collegiate dictionary contains approximately 60,000 words. However, the average college graduate has a vocabulary of less than 10,000 words. The majority of English language words are articles, prepositions, conjunctions, adjectives, verbs, and adverbs. Noun words only represent a fraction of the total number of vocabulary words. If the average college graduate only uses 2,000 to 3,000 nouns, how many nouns, or *entities,* are necesary to represent the *data elements* within our companies or our data processing systems?

The majority of data names used in data processing systems are homonyms, synonyms, and aliases of a relatively few unique entities. These synonyms and aliases were created because of the lack of naming standards or the lack of planning concerning the creation and use of data elements. They were created by a multitude of programmers and analysts who labeled their own data, without regard for the way others had named the same data.

The thousands of names used in our data processing systems can be reduced to a relatively few *"core" data elements.* This is illustrated in the example below.

Within our data processing systems, a data element such as EMPLOYEE-NAME is often given multiple labels. Some of the labels might include:

EMP-NAME
E-NAME
NAME-OF-EMPLOYEE
EMPL-NAME
EMPLOYEE-NM
EMP-NM

Likewise, the names of other persons affiliated or associated with the company are also given different names such as:

ASSOCIATE-NAME
BUYER-NAME
CLIENT-NAME
CUSTOMER-NAME
FOREMAN-NAME
MANAGER-NAME
SUPERVISOR-NAME
SUPPLIER-NAME
VENDOR-NAME

However, all of these names could be represented by a few simple data elements. These data elements would be as follows:

- PERSON-NAME: The name designated and used by a human being.
- PERSON-TYPE-CODE: 1 = associate; 2 = buyer; 3 = client; 4 = customer; 5 = employee; etc.
- PERSON-NAME-TYPE-CODE: 1 = first name; 2 = middle name; 3 = last name.

Thus, it is possible to greatly simplify and reduce the total number of data elements used within our data processing systems. This can be achieved by constructing a relatively few elemental "atomic" data elements from which all other data can be derived.

A Foundation for Standardized Data Elements By adhering to the following rules, we can construct a foundation of standardized data elements from which accurate and reliable information can be derived.

Rule 1: Define a data element in such a way that the definition of this entity can be adequately described in a single simple sentence.

Journalists are trained to summarize or describe a news event in one sentence. This summary typically is the first sentence of any newspaper article. This summary sentence contains the following constructs to describe any news event:

- Who
- What
- When
- Where
- How much

For example, the following sentence could be used to introduce or summarize a news article describing a fire. *On Tuesday, May 18, 1981, at 10:05 AM, the Sam Smith residence at 1801 Main Street, Chicago, burned to the ground.* This single sentence answers the following questions:

- Who? (Sam Smith)
- What? (residence . . . burned)
- When? (Tuesday, May 18, 1981, at 10:05 AM)
- Where? (1801 Main Street, Chicago)
- How much? (to the ground)

This same principle should be applied to the description or definition of data elements. By designing data elements that can be defined with a single statement, we can assure ourselves that these data elements are elemental, cohesive ones. For a further consideration of cohesive data elements, see Data Coupling and Cohesion, later in this chapter. By designing simple, elemental data entities, we are maximizing the utility or usefulness of these entities throughout all of our data processing systems.

For example, the following data element is not an elemental one.

Data element: DELIVERY-DISPOSITION-CODE

Format: 999X9999

Description: Identifies the distribution or drop-off points for truck deliveries from the warehouse. The deliveries are then picked up by wholesale or retail buyers. The first three digits identify the city. For example: 001 = Chicago; 002 = Denver; etc. The fourth digit describes the type of material being delivered (A = fragile; B = perishable; C = clothing; D = machinery). Positions five through eight identify the wholesale or retail buyers. 0001–5000 = retail; 5001–9999 = wholesale. Even numbers are used for C.O.D. buyers and odd numbers are used for credit buyers.

This data element actually contains the following information:

- CITY CODE (Chicago, Denver, etc.)
- MATERIAL TYPE (fragile, perishable, etc.)
- BUYER TYPE (retail, wholesale)
- BUYER PAYMENT TERMS (C.O.D., credit)

Therefore, the information portrayed within the single data element DELIVERY-DISPOSITION-CODE should have been accomplished by constructing four separate data entities.

Rule 2: Whenever possible, use combinations or concatenations of generic data elements to identify specific entities.

In biology a classification scheme is employed to identify any member of the plant or animal kingdom. By using this taxonomy, any plant or animal can be accurately identified by using only eight constructs. The eight constructs are as follows:

- Kingdom
  - Division
    - Subdivision
      - Order

- Family
  - Genus
    - Species
      - Variety

By employing this naming convention, we can focus in on any specific entity by identifying the various levels of qualifications or categories in which the entity is found. This *funneling* or channeling concept can also be used to accurately name, identify, and classify data elements within our data processing systems.

This concept employs levels of qualification ordered from generic, or general, categories to specific categories. The first or highest level of qualification should be the *class word.* Class words are used to categorize entities by their use within data processing systems. Below are the recommended class words to be used to identify the generic classification for a data entity.

AMOUNT	NAME
CODE	NUMBER
CONSTANT	PERCENT
COUNT	TEXT
DATE	TIME

The subsequent or lower levels of qualification depend on the type of entity being identified. The example in Table 3-3 illustrates the use of multiple data elements to identify specific data classifications concerning EMPLOYEE information.

Table 3-3

Level	*Entity category*
1	CLASS-WORD-TYPE (amount, code, date, etc.)
2	NAME-TYPE (person, building, company, etc.)
3	PERSON-TYPE (employee, client, vendor, etc.)
4	EMPLOYEE-TYPE (part-time, full-time, etc.)
5	EMPLOYEE-JOB-TYPE (clerical, engineer, etc.)
6	ENGINEER-EXPERIENCE-TYPE (aircraft, bridge, automobile, etc.)

Figure 3-2 illustrates the successive levels of qualification that could be used to identify employee personnel information.

By employing this data element identification scheme, we are using a naming technique consistent with data retrieval or search arguments.

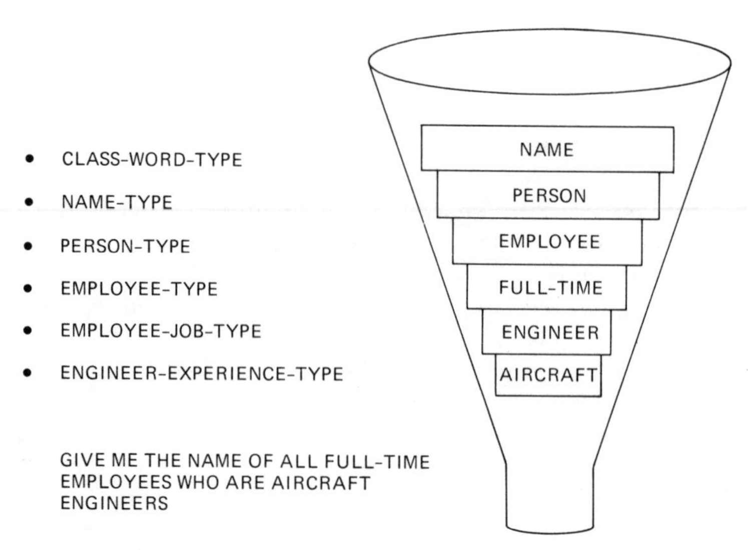

Fig. 3-2 Taxonomy of data.

For example, this naming scheme can be effectively used to satisfy the following user query:

GIVE ME THE NAME OF ALL FULL-TIME EMPLOYEES WHO ARE AIRCRAFT ENGINEERS.

Unless we utilize a data naming convention compatible and consistent with data search techniques, the results of the search may be unreliable or unpredictable. We cannot minimize the possibility of data search and update anomalies unless we can first minimize the possibility of naming and identification anomalies.

Rule 3: Develop and use standardized and consistent attributes to qualify or categorize data entities.

Below are some suggested adjectives that can be used to describe some standard classifications for data entities:

Extreme Qualifiers: maximum/minimum
lowest/highest
least/most
longest/shortest

Positional Qualifiers: first, second, third . . . middle, last
beginning/ending

Time Qualifiers: hourly, daily, weekly, monthly, quarterly, annually
week-to-date, month-to-date, year-to-date

Consistency is the rule of thumb when designating data name qualifiers. For example, there are many synonyms or optional words that could be used to indicate the beginning and ending of a time period. Table 3-4 illustrates this principle.

Table 3-4

Beginning	*Ending*	*Context*
arrival	departure	journey
hire, start	separation, termination	employment
go	stop	motion
active	inactive	activity

Why not simply use the words BEGINNING (BEG) and ENDING (END) in place of the above synonyms?

Rule 4: Minimize the use of specific data element names; rather, maximize the use of roles or domain to specify exactness.

Movie actors play different roles in different movies. For example, John Wayne could play a cavalry soldier in one movie, and a wagon train leader in the next. Data also play different roles. Normally these roles are *time dependent* or *location dependent.* Table 3-5 is an example of a data entity that is both *time and location dependent.* This example illustrates the various tags or names used to label subjects as they evolve through a typical criminal justice system.

Table 3-5

Data name	*Description*
SUSPECT-NAME	The name of a person suspected of involvement in a crime
DEFENDANT-NAME	The name of a person accused of participation in a crime
CRIMINAL-NAME	The name of a person who has been convicted of a crime
PRISONER-NAME	The name of a person confined in a penal institution for committing a crime
PAROLEE-NAME	The name of a person who has been released from a penal institution

A preferred alternative to creating five specific data elements is to design two generic data elements:

- SUBJECT-NAME: The name of a person involved in the justice process
- WHERE ROLES: 1 = suspect; 2 = defendant; 3 = criminal; 4 = prisoner; 5 = parolee

There are several advantages to minimizing the use of specific or exact data element names and maximizing the use of codes or roles. These advantages include:

- Reducing the total number of data element names and the complexity of the data processing system. As the preceding example illustrated, the number of data elements was reduced by 80 percent.
- Increasing the modularity or usefulness of the entity, by codifying the various uses or roles of the entities. For example, in a criminal justice system, there may be different files or programs devoted to specific phases in which a subject is being processed. For example, there may be a SUSPECT-MASTER-FILE and a CRIMINAL-MASTER-FILE. However, a data element such as SUBJECT-NAME can be used regardless of the physical storage location or the particular application system.
- Reducing future maintenance costs. Often government legislation mandates changes to our legal systems. If the legal qualifications of a suspect or a criminal change, it is possible that we could accommodate this change merely by modifying the values of the roles and not the data element names themselves. Also, if additional phases or roles are introduced to the justice process, we need only add more roles without affecting the data element names.

Rule 5: When labeling data elements, maximize the logical constructs and minimize the physical constructs.

Data elements can have both logical and physical attributes. Logical characteristics answer the question What, while data element roles or values should be used to identify Where, When, Who, and How much.

Whenever possible, the data element itself should only describe What, while data element roles or values should be used to identify Where, When, Who, and How much.

For example, the data element name CURRENT-EMPLOYEE-DATABASE-RECORD-STATUS could be used to hold a code which identifies the condition of this record, where 1 = active, 2 = inactive, and 3 = delete. However, this data element name also describes When (CURRENT) and Where

(EMPLOYEE DATABASE). This severely restricts the modularity or flexibility of the data element. A preferred method is to construct a data element whose name describes What, and build other data elements whose roles or values define When and Where.

- WHAT: DATABASE-RECORD-STATUS = The state or condition of a database record, where 1 = active; 2 = inactive; and 3 = delete.
- WHEN: GENERATION-CODE = A code that identifies a relative time period, where 1 = previous; 2 = current; and 3 = next.
- WHERE: DATABASE-TYPE-CODE = A code that identifies the contents of the data structure, where 1 = employee; 2 = manufacturing; and 3 = sales.

In summary, there are several techniques that can be utilized to increase the effectiveness and decrease the complexity of our use of data. To utilize these techniques, we must adopt disciplines in the way we name, classify, and identify data. This taxonomy of data is essential if we are to use database technology to achieve our goal of providing the world with accurate, inexpensive information.

DA Standards for COBOL

The following sections specifically apply to data usage considerations within the COBOL language.

COBOL Condition-Name Standards COBOL condition names (88-level names) are a dilemma to data administration. The disadvantage of 88-level names is that by using them, we are creating alias names for the group name they modify. The advantage of 88-level names is that they eliminate the need to "hard code" constants in a program. Thus, they provide for more consistent and global data use. They also provide the means to map the use of constants or literal values throughout a system. Because of this, DA should encourage the use of 88-level names. However, the following standards should be adhered to when designing data elements that use condition names.

1. All 88-level names should be documented in and extracted from the data dictionary. By doing so, they can be available for use throughout all systems.
2. The originator of 88-level names for a data element should define *all* values used for that data element. This is important, so that all possible codes can be documented and available for companywide use.

Incomplete

```
01  EMPLOYEE-RECORD.
    05  EMPLOYEE-MINORITY-CODE         PIC X.
        88  CAUCASIAN                  VALUE '0'.
        88  BLACK                      VALUE '1'.
```

Better

```
01  EMPLOYEE-RECORD.
    05  EMPLOYEE-MINORITY-CODE         PIC X.
        88  CAUCASIAN                  VALUE '0'.
        88  BLACK                      VALUE '1'.
        88  ORIENTAL                   VALUE '3'.
        88  ASIAN                      VALUE '4'.
        88  INDIAN                     VALUE '5'.
        88  LATIN                      VALUE '6'.
        88  HISPANIC                   VALUE '8'.
```

3. The 88-level names should only be used with data elements whose range of values (domain) is static, not dynamic. Examples of each follow.

Static: STATE-CODE
MINORITY-CODE

Dynamic: ACCOUNT-NUMBER
CHARGE-NUMBER

In other words, 88-levels should not be used with data that changes frequently. If we create 88-level names for data elements whose domain changes frequently, we will create a severe maintenance problem for the dictionary and the programs that use these data elements.

4. Only data names with a limited number of values should be described by 88-level names. For example, EMPLOYEE-MINORITY-CODE has a limited (or manageable) number of values.

```
01  EMPLOYEE-INFORMATION.
    05  EMPLOYEE-MINORITY-CODE         PIC X.
        88  CAUCASIAN                  VALUE '0'.
        88  BLACK                      VALUE '1'
        88  ORIENTAL                   VALUE '3'.
```

```
88  ASIAN                         VALUE '4'.
88  INDIAN                        VALUE '5'.
88  LATIN                         VALUE '6'.
88  HISPANIC                      VALUE '8'.
```

As a general rule, do not create 88-levels for data elements with more than 50 values. U.S. State Code (50 states) is a good rule of thumb.

5. The 88-level names should conform to the same rules as any other data names.

Incomplete

```
05  EMP-MINORITY-CD
    88  CAUCASIAN
    88  BLACK
    88  ORIENTAL
    88  ASIAN
    88  INDIAN
    88  LATIN
    88  HISPANIC
```

Better

```
05  EMP-MINORITY-CD
    88  EMP-MINORITY-CAUCASIAN-CD
    88  EMP-MINORITY-BLACK-CD
    88  EMP-MINORITY-ORIENTAL-CD
    88  EMP-MINORITY-ASIAN-CD
    88  EMP-MINORITY-INDIAN-CD
    88  EMP-MINORITY-LATIN-CD
    88  EMP-MINORITY-HISPANIC-CD
```

Whenever possible, link the 88-level name to the name of the data element being described.

COBOL Redefinition Standards From a data administration viewpoint, there is a right and a wrong way to use the REDEFINES clause. Let us consider the various uses of the COBOL REDEFINES clause. The following is an example of the proper use of the REDEFINES clause:

```
01  STATE-ABBREV-TABLE.
    05  FILLER        PIC X(02) VALUE 'AK'.
    05  FILLER        PIC X(02) VALUE 'AL'.
```

```
    05 FILLER        PIC X(02) VALUE 'AZ'.
    05 FILLER        PIC X(02) VALUE 'AR'.
    05 FILLER        PIC X(02) VALUE 'CA'.
    05 FILLER        PIC X(02) VALUE 'CO'.
    05 FILLER        PIC X(02) VALUE 'CT'.
    05 FILLER        PIC X(02) VALUE 'DE'.
          .                 .
          .                 .
          .                 .

01 STATE-ABBREV-TABLE-REDF REDEFINES STATE-ABBREV-TABLE.
    05 STATE-ENTRY          PIC X(02)
       OCCURS 50 TIMES
       INDEXED BY STATE-INDEX.
```

In this example, the REDEFINES clause is needed to locate a particular value for multiple occurrences of a data element within a table.

However, REDEFINES clauses are sometimes used unnecessarily. Below is an example of the indiscriminate use of the REDEFINES clause.

```
01 ZIP-CODE                              PIC 9(5).
01 ZIP-CODE-REDF REDEFINES ZIP-CODE      PIC X(5).
```

Is it really necessary to define ZIP-CODE as both numeric and alphanumeric? Since it is highly unlikely that ZIP-CODE will be used in an arithmetic computation, there is no need to create this data element with a numeric PICTURE clause. By simply defining ZIP-CODE as PIC X(5), we eliminate the need for a redefinition.

Here is another questionable use of the REDEFINES clause.

```
01 LAST-MAINTENANCE-DATE.
    05 LAST-MAINT-MONTH          PIC 99.
    05 LAST-MAINT-DAY            PIC 99.
    05 LAST-MAINT-YEAR           PIC 99.
01 LAST-MAINT-DATE-REDF REDEFINES
   LAST-MAINTENANCE-DATE         PIC X(6).
```

Unless the month, day, and year fields above will be used in an arithmetic calculation, there is no need to define these data elements with numeric formats. Below is a simpler, preferred version of this data definition.

```
01 LAST-MAINTENANCE-DATE.
    05 LAST-MAINT-MONTH         PIC XX.
    05 LAST-MAINT-DAY           PIC XX.
    05 LAST-MAINT-YEAR          PIC XX.
```

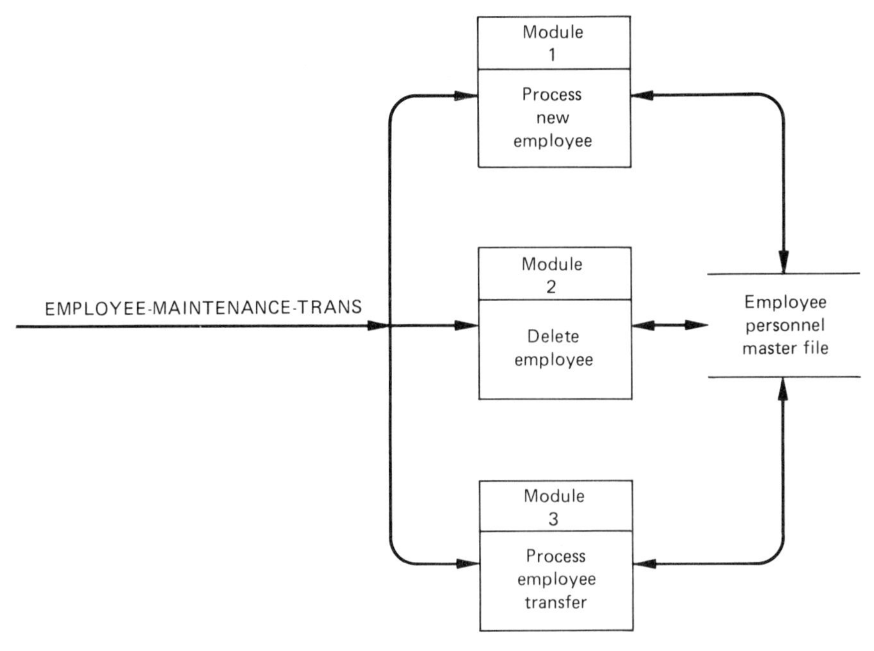

Fig. 3-3 Data definition coupling.

Data should be designed to minimize coupling and maximize modularity. The example in Figure 3-3 illustrates how a REDEFINES clause can increase data coupling and decrease data modularity.

The data definition below describes payroll transactions to add, delete, or modify information on the employee personnel master file.

```
01  EMPLOYEE-MAINTENANCE-TRANS.
    05  TRANSACTION-CODE                PIC X.
    05  EMPLOYEE-NUMBER                 PIC X(5).
    05  ADD-EMPLOYEE-DATA.
        10  EMPLOYEE-NAME               PIC X(25).
        10  EMPLOYEE-ADDRESS            PIC X(20).
        10  CITY-NAME                   PIC X(20).
        10  STATE-CODE                  PIC X(2).
        10  ZIP-CODE                    PIC X(5).
        10  SEX                         PIC X.
        10  MINORITY-CODE               PIC X.
    05  DELETE-EMPLOYEE-DATA REDEFINES ADD-EMPLOYEE-DATA.
        10  DELETE-CODE                 PIC X.
        10  DELETE-EFFECTIVE-DATE       PIC X(6).
        10  FILLER                      PIC X(67).
    05  TRANSFER-EMPLOYEE-DATA REDEFINES ADD-EMPLOYEE-DATA.
        10  TRANSFER-FROM-LOCATION      PIC X(3).
        10  TRANSFER-TO-LOCATION        PIC X(3).
```

```
        10  TRANSFER-REASON-CODE          PIC XX.
        10  TRANSFER-MONTH                PIC XX.
        10  TRANSFER-DAY                  PIC XX.
        10  TRANSFER-YEAR                 PIC XX.
        10  FILLER                        PIC X(60).
```

There are several disadvantages to this data definition.

1. All three transaction formats are coupled together into one data definition. Therefore, a change in the format of any transaction will affect the entire data description.
2. Even if a program uses only one transaction, the data definition for all three transaction types must be included in the source code for that program.
3. This data definition maximizes the likelihood that a change in this data definition will require a change to multiple programs. Thus, we are increasing the cost of future program maintenance as a result of a change in data design. The data flow diagram in Figure 3-3 illustrates this coupling of data format. In the diagram, three different programs are used to process employee adds, employee deletes, and employee transfers. If a change is made to any transaction format, we must recompile all three programs.

Below is the preferred data definition for EMPLOYEE-MAINTENANCE-TRANS.

```
01  EMPLOYEE-MAINTENANCE-TRANS.
    05  TRANSACTION-CODE          PIC X.
    05  EMPLOYEE-NUMBER           PIC X(5).
    05  FILLER                    PIC X(74).
01  ADD-EMPLOYEE-TRANS.
    05  FILLER                    PIC X(6).
    05  EMPLOYEE-NAME             PIC X(25).
    05  EMPLOYEE-ADDRESS          PIC X(20).
    05  CITY-NAME                 PIC X(20).
    05  STATE-CODE                PIC X(2).
    05  ZIP-CODE                  PIC X(5).
    05  SEX                       PIC X.
    05  MINORITY-CODE             PIC X.
01  DELETE-EMPLOYEE-TRANS.
    05  FILLER                    PIC X(6).
    05  DELETE-CODE               PIC X.
    05  DELETE-EFFECTIVE-DATE     PIC X(6).
    05  FILLER                    PIC X(67).
```

```
01  TRANSFER-EMPLOYEE-TRANS.
    05  FILLER                     PIC X(6).
    05  TRANSFER-FROM-LOCATION     PIC X(3).
    05  TRANSFER-TO-LOCATION       PIC X(3).
    05  TRANSFER-REASON-CODE       PIC XX.
    05  TRANSFER-MONTH             PIC XX.
    05  TRANSFER-DAY               PIC XX.
    05  TRANSFER-YEAR              PIC XX.
    05  FILLER                     PIC X(60).
```

By eliminating the use of the REDEFINES, we have decoupled the data and thus restored the modularity of the data definition. Furthermore, we have isolated the key data elements common to all three transaction types. The data flow diagram in Figure 3-4 illustrates this more modular data design.

The elimination of the divergent input data flow indicates that these data definitions have been decoupled. By fragmenting the input data flows, we have minimized the possibility that a change in any one transaction format will have an impact on more than one program. This minimizes future program maintenance costs resulting from a change in the data format.

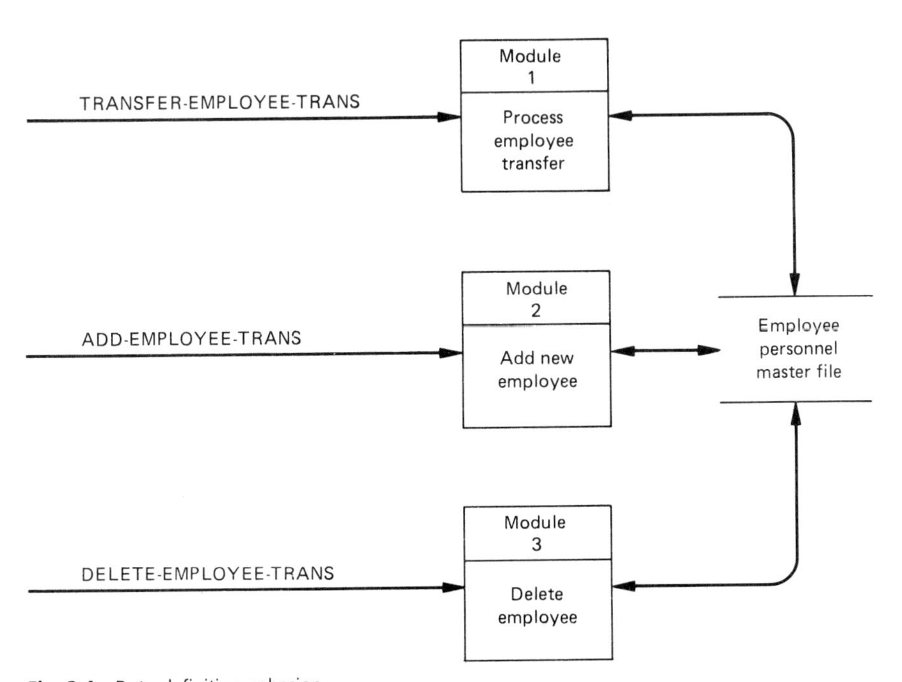

Fig. 3-4 Data definition cohesion.

There are, however, some disadvantages to this data design. The program using this data must contain the data definition for the key fields (EMPLOYEE-MAINTENANCE-TRANS) and the data definition for the detail data (e.g., ADD-EMPLOYEE-TRANS). If multiple transactions are used in one program, the program must first interrogate the contents of EMPLOYEE-MAINTENANCE-TRANS to determine the transaction type, then move this record to the appropriate transaction data definition (ADD-EMPLOYEE-TRANS, DELETE-EMPLOYEE-TRANS, or TRANSFER-EMPLOYEE-TRANS). However, the modularity gained from this data design outweighs these disadvantages.

Consistency Standards

Wherever possible, it is important to maintain consistency among the words used in related data names. For example, data elements referring to DATE often identify the beginning or ending of a time period. The beginning and ending dates could be named with the words BEG- and END- or with START- and STOP- and so forth. The choice of BEG- and END- or of START- and STOP- makes little difference. However, if BEG- and END- are chosen to be the standard to indicate the beginning and ending of a time period, then they should be used with every applicable data element name.

It is also important to maintain consistency of certain class words. The class words ID, INDICATOR, IDENTIFIER, FLAG, and CODE have similar purposes. All such data elements should be named as CODE or CD (abbreviation). The reasons for this are explained below.

Programmers and others often use both FLAGS and CODES to indicate condition parameters. Since a FLAG is used to indicate one of two conditions, and a CODE indicates one of several conditions, a CODE is a more flexible, comprehensive entity type than FLAG. Also, we want to eliminate the need to change a data name from FLAG to CODE if the values of a given data element are expanded. For example, let us assume that the data element EMPLOYEE-STATUS-FLAG is used to indicate the employment status of an employee. The two valid values of this data element are:

A = active

T = terminated

Let us assume that the company changes the payroll policy to permit employees to take an extended leave of absence. It is now necessary to add a third value to EMPLOYEE-STATUS-FLAG:

A = active

T = terminated

L = leave of absence

Although this data element now is a CODE-type entity, it would be expensive to change all occurrences of this data element from EMPLOYEE-STATUS-FLAG to EMPLOYEE-STATUS-CODE. Therefore, the word FLAG should be avoided in a data name. All INDICATOR-type entities should be assigned a class word of CODE.

Whenever possible, the attributes (length, format) of a data element should be consistent with the classification of the entity.

Example:

Class word	*Possible standard format*
DATE (DT)	YYMMDD
PERCENT (PCT)	9V9999*

*1.0000 = 100%   0.9900 = 99%

By maintaining consistency of attributes, we can avoid several versions and aliases of data names that might arise from variations in the format of the data entities. This will also minimize the need to reformat or convert one data format to another.

For those data element names that contain a verb, always use the present tense of the verb. For example, the following names represent different tenses or spellings of verbs.

EMPLOYEE-LAST-DAY-WORKED
EMPLOYEE-LAST-DAY-WORKS
EMPLOYEE-LAST-DAY-WORK

Also, as a general rule, always use the singular, not the plural, representation of a word. In the example above, the preferred data element name would be

EMPLOYEE-LAST-DAY-WORK

In COBOL, use only numeric (9) and alphanumeric (X) formats for data entities. Never use the alphabetic format (A), even if the entity is always alphabetic.

Example: Do not use ⟶ EMPLOYEE-MIDDLE-INITIAL PIC A.
Use instead ⟶ EMPLOYEE-MIDDLE-INITIAL PIC X.

Use the 9 format only with data elements involved in arithmetic operations. Maximize the use of the X format, since this is the most flexible format attribute of a data name.

Example: HIRE-DATE PIC X(06).
LAST-SALARY-AMOUNT PIC S9(6)V99.

Automated Tools to Assist in Enforcing DA Naming Conventions

The data element naming standards described in previous sections have the potential to increase the quality and effectiveness of the data resource. However, without suitable means to detect and correct violations in naming standards, this potential will not be realized. Traditionally, data administration has audited data dictionary input on an informal or random spot-checking basis, a very inaccurate and time-consuming process. It is difficult, if not impossible, for the DA staff to manually or visually scan new data elements for compliance with naming conventions. For the data administrator to manually scan each new data element for the existence of one of an organization's hundreds or thousands of prime words (or its standard abbreviation) would be an unreasonable burden. The only practical means for the data administrator to enforce naming conventions is to use an automated tool such as the automated DA Naming Standard Auditor available from Data Administration, Inc. Figure 3-5 shows a sample printout. This tool is able to detect and notify the data administrator of 20 different violations in DA naming standards:

1. *Class words* This utility will detect the absence of a class word within the data element name. These class words are installation-defined.
2. *Prime words* This utility will notify the data administrator if no prime word is found in the data element name. These prime words are user-defined.
3. *Standard abbreviations* If desired, this utility will substitute fully spelled words within a data element name with their standard abbreviation counterparts from a user-defined standard abbreviation list. By automatically substituting standard abbreviations for fully spelled words, the data administrator can be assured that data element names will not consist of combinations of fully spelled words and standard abbreviations. This facility helps to decrease the length of a data element name.
4. *Synonyms* This facility can also be used to substitute synonyms with installation-recognized standard words for these synonyms. As illustrated in Figure 3-6, this utility can be used to eliminate the synonyms WORKER, ASSOC, and ASSOCIATE by substituting the installation standard abbreviation EMP (employee). Synonym replacement is accomplished by an installation-defined substitution table.
5. *Prefixes* If desired, this utility will compare the first word in a data element name against a user-defined prefix list. If no match is found, DA will be notified of the violation.

NAMECHEK ERROR REPORT

NAME/WORD IN ERROR	ERROR CODE	ERROR MESSAGE	ERROR POSITION
ACCT-NO-DTE	075	THIS NAME DOES NOT CONTAIN A CLASS WORD	01
	050	THIS NAME DOES NOT CONTAIN A PRIME WORD	01
	950	NAME IS UNACCEPTABLE - WRITTEN TO INVALID OUT FILE	
AN-ILLEGAL-WORD	375	THIS WORD IS AN ILLEGAL WORD	01
AN	075	THIS NAME DOES NOT CONTAIN A CLASS WORD	01
	050	THIS NAME DOES NOT CONTAIN A PRIME WORD	01
	950	NAME IS UNACCEPTABLE - WRITTEN TO INVALID OUT FILE	
DT-COMPLETED	050	THIS NAME DOES NOT CONTAIN A PRIME WORD	01
	950	NAME IS UNACCEPTABLE - WRITTEN TO INVALID OUT FILE	
IN-DT-1	400	THIS WORD IS TOO SHORT - NUMBER OF CHARACTERS IS 1	07
1	050	THIS NAME DOES NOT CONTAIN A PRIME WORD	01
	950	NAME IS UNACCEPTABLE - WRITTEN TO INVALID OUT FILE	
NBR-UNACCEPTABLE-ERRORS	425	THIS WORD IS TOO LONG - NUMBER OF CHARACTERS IS 12	05
UNACCEPTABLE	050	THIS NAME DOES NOT CONTAIN A PRIME WORD	01
	950	NAME IS UNACCEPTABLE - WRITTEN TO INVALID OUT FILE	
IN-1	400	THIS WORD IS TOO SHORT - NUMBER OF CHARACTERS IS 1	04
1	100	THIS NAME IS TOO SHORT - LENGTH IN CHARACTERS IS 4	01
	075	THIS NAME DOES NOT CONTAIN A CLASS WORD	01
	050	THIS NAME DOES NOT INCLUDE A PRIME WORD	01
	950	NAME IS UNACCEPTABLE - WRITTEN TO INVALID OUT FILE	
EMPLOYEE-SOCIAL-SECURITY-NO	075	THIS NAME DOES NOT CONTAIN A CLASS WORD	01
	950	NAME IS UNACCEPTABLE - WRITTEN TO INVALID OUT FILE	
STATUS	150	THIS NAME HAS TOO FEW WORDS - NUMBER OF WORDS IS 1	01
	075	THIS NAME DOES NOT CONTAIN A CLASS WORD	01
	050	THIS NAME DOES NOT CONTAIN A PRIME WORD	01
	950	NAME IS UNACCEPTABLE - WRITTEN TO INVALID OUT FILE	
NBR-OF-WORDS-IN-A-DATA-NAME	375	THIS WORD IS AN ILLEGAL WORD	17
A	400	THIS WORD IS TOO SHORT - NUMBER OF CHARACTERS IS 1	17
A	175	THIS NAME HAS TOO MANY WORDS - NUMBER OF WORDS IS 7	01
	050	THIS NAME DOES NOT CONTAIN A PRIME WORD	01

Fig. 3-5 Sample printout from DA Naming Standard Auditor.

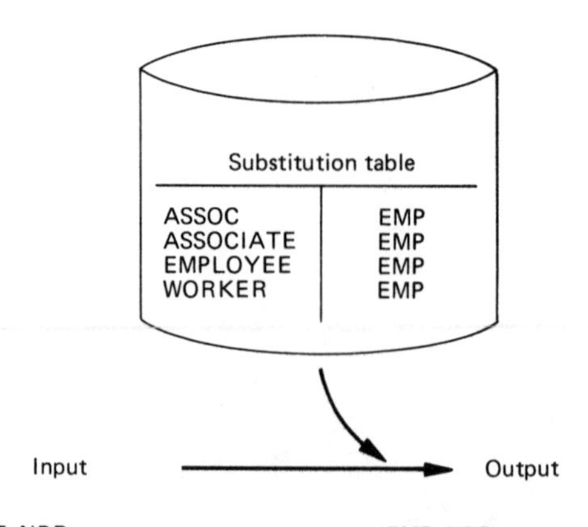

Fig. 3-6 Installation-defined substitution table.

6. *Suffixes* This facility will also compare the last word in a data element name against the installation-defined suffix list. If no match is found, DA will be notified.
7. *The position of a class word* Some installations have the standard requiring the class word to be the first or the last word in a name. If desired, this software package will audit for this.
8. *The position of a prime word* If desired, this utility will notify DA if the prime word is not the first or the last word within a data name.
9. *Illegal words* Illegal words are words that the data administrator may want to prohibit from use in data element names. Such illegal words could be certain English language articles, prepositions, or conjunctions that add little or no meaning to the data element name. Below are examples of possible illegal words.

Possible Illegal Words

Articles	*Conjunctions*	*Prepositions*
A	AND	IN
AN	BUT	THROUGH
THE	OR	THRU
	NOR	
	FOR	
	AS	
	AFTER	
	BECAUSE	
	IF	
	WHEN	

10. *Illegal names* Illegal names are certain names that DA may want to prohibit from use. If your installation is a COBOL shop, this installation-defined illegal names table could include COBOL reserved names. Below is an example of such a table:

Possible Illegal Names
CLOCK-UNITS
COM-REG
DAY-OF-WEEK
DB-STATUS
FILE-LIMITS
MORE-LABELS
NUMERIC-EDITED
RECORD-OVERFLOW
SORT-MESSAGE

11. *The minimum number of words in a data element name* To assure that data element names are descriptive and meaningful, DA may want to set a minimum number of words allowed in a data element name. For example, the data administrator may decide that all data element names must have at least two words. This utility would then detect and notify DA of any names that did not have at least two words.
12. *The maximum number of words in a data element name* To assure that data element names are not too long or cumbersome for use by programmers and end users, DA may set a limit on the maximum number of words allowed in a name.
13. *The minimum number of characters allowed in a data element name* This facility can be used in conjunction with item 11, above.
14. *The maximum number of characters allowed in a data element name* This parameter can be helpful in controlling the length of a data element name. For example, the maximum allowable length for COBOL alias names would be 30 characters.
15. *The minimum number of characters allowed in each word in a data element name* DA probably does not want to permit the use of one-character words in data element names. The presence of one-character words could indicate a violation in first normal form (see Normalization Standards, later in this chapter). For example, the data names EMP-DEPENDENT-1 and EMPLOYEE-DEPENDENT-2 could be a symptom of repetitive data groupings, and thus a data structure that does not meet the requirements of first normal form. By using this utility, data administrators can gain some insight into the quality of data structure design.
16. *The maximum number of characters allowed in each word in a name* By restricting the number of characters allowed in each word, DA can

be notified when there is a need to create a standard abbreviation for a fully spelled word. For example, words over 8 or 10 characters (such as MANUFACTURING and CLASSIFICATION) should be abbreviated.

17. *Words that are all numerics.*
18. *Words that contain one or more numeric characters* As explained in item 15, above, the use of numeric characters such as EMPLOYEE-DEP1 and PART-ITEM3 could be an indication of a repeating data group and a possible violation of first normal form. NAMECHEK will notify DA of any such violations.
19. *Words that are plural spellings* NAMECHEK will assist in identifying words that are plural spellings. It is important that the data administrator maintain consistency of spelling of data element names and not mix singular and plural spellings.
20. *Acronyms* NAMECHEK will scan data element names for the existence of installation-defined valid or acceptable acronyms such as I-B-M, Z-I-P, or C-O-D. If single-character word strings are detected that are not valid acronyms, NAMECHEK will notify the data administrator.

Standard Abbreviations and Acronyms

The previously mentioned COBOL naming standards tend to significantly increase the length of a data name. This is unpopular among those who must use these data names in system documentation. This is also unpopular among programmers who must code programs using long data names. These data names are significantly longer than the mnemonic names programmers have traditionally assigned themselves. In some cases, long data names can require the use of two lines of COBOL code for a simple MOVE or IF statement. To minimize these problems, wherever possible the words should be abbreviated within the data name. However, it is important to establish standards for the abbreviations of words.

Data administration should lead the effort in creating a standard abbreviation list for the entire organization. Choosing the correct standard abbreviation to use should be based on the popularity of its use. It is important to get representatives from all areas of the enterprise to review and approve standard abbreviations. For example, should a company use NUM or NBR as the standard abbreviation for NUMBER?

When creating the standard abbreviation list for initial review, the following standards should be used;

1. Many abbreviations can be created simply by removing vowels from the fully spelled words.

Example:

AMOUNT	AMNT
CODE	CD
DATE	DT
HEADER	HDR
NAME	NM
NUMBER	NMBR

See the next section, Automating the Foundation for Naming Standards, for a discussion of automated tools to create standard abbreviation lists.

2. As many data processing and user areas as possible should be involved in the review and approval of standard abbreviations. When there is a conflict between user areas over which abbreviation to use for a given word, consult a standard abbreviation and acronym reference manual. Some reference texts are *Acronyms, Initialisms, and Abbreviations Dictionary,* 7th edition (available from Gale Research Co., Book Tower, Detroit, Michigan 48226) and *Military Standard Abbreviations* (MIL-STD-ASD) and the *U.S. Government Printing Office Style Manual,* revised edition (both available from the U.S. Government Printing Office, 710 N. Capitol Street, N.W., Washington, D.C. 20402).
3. Do not create acronyms or abbreviations that are English words:

Example:

Word	***Proposed abbreviation***
Participate/participation	PART
Allow/allowance/allowable	ALL
Number	NO
Foreign	FOR

There are two exceptions to this rule, however: IN can be used for input and OUT can be used for output.

It is important to follow this rule in order to minimize the possibility of anomalies during automated queries or searches of data element names. For example, the data elements NO-TRANSACTIONS and NO-INPUT-CODE (in this instance NO connotates NOTHING or NONE) have nothing in common with PART-NO (in this instance NO means NUMBER) even though all three would be the output of a search for all names that contained the word NO.

4. If a standard abbreviation for a word exists, always use it. Thus, do not create data element names with a mixture of fully spelled words and their abbreviated counterparts.

Example:

Do not use	***Use instead***
EMPLOYEE-PAYROLL-NUMBER	EMP-PYRL-NBR
EMP-SOCIAL-SEC-NUMBER	EMP-SOC-SEC-NBR

This will not only improve the accuracy of automated searches, but will also reduce the length of a data name. This standard will help ease the pain among those programmers opposed to longer, more meaningful data names.

If the data processing and user community within your installation seek to minimize the length of data element names, you may want to adopt the IBM-recognized symbolic abbreviations for class words. Figure 3-7 is a list of the IBM-recognized class word symbols.

5. Do not choose standard abbreviations for your company that conflict with abbreviations used commonly outside your company.

Example:

Word group	*Possible abbreviation*	*Preferred abbreviation*
Taxable	TX	TXBL
Code	COD	CD

Use TXBL instead of TX, since TX is the standard U.S. Postal Service abbreviation for Texas. Use CD instead of COD, since COD is a common acronym for *C*ash *o*n *D*elivery.

6. Preferably, the abbreviation of a word should begin with the same letters as the word being abbreviated.

Example:

Word group	*Possible abbreviation*	*Preferred abbreviation*
Christmas	XMAS	CRSTMS
Cross-reference	XREF	CROSSREF

By doing so, an abbreviation can be easily associated with its full-word counterpart in a cross-reference (keyword) index listing. (See Automated Redundancy Auditing Tools in Chapter 4 for an explanation of keyword index listings.)

7. All data element names created within an enterprise should conform to the established standard abbreviation conventions.

Automating the Foundation for Naming Standards

Before data administration can apply naming standards against entity names, DA should create at least three categories or classifications of words. These three categories are class words, prime words, and standard abbreviations. Class words are fairly common among all organizations and are limited to a very few words (see Data Element Naming Standards, above). However, prime words and standard abbreviations vary considerably from one organization to the next and can involve hundreds (often thousands) of entries. How can the data administrator develop and manage such a large number of prime words and standard

SYMBOL	CLASS WORD	DEFINITION	EXAMPLE
N	NAME	ALPHABETIC DATA WHICH IDENTIFIES SPECIFIC ENTITIES.	CUSTOMER NAME SUPPLIER NAME
#	NUMBER	ALPHA-NUMERIC DATA WHICH IDENTIFIES SPECIFIC ENTITIES.	PURCHASE ORDER NUMBER PART NUMBER
C	CODE	DATA WHICH IDENTIFIES CLASSIFICATIONS OF ENTITIES.	SHIPMENT OF STATUS CODE UNIT OF MEASURE CODE
Q	COUNT (QUANTITY)	THE NUMBER OR QUANTITY (INCLUDING FRACTIONS) OF ANYTHING EXCEPT MONETARY AMOUNTS.	QUANTITY ORDERED QUANTITY RECEIVED
$	AMOUNT (CURRENCY)	THE QUANTITY OF MONETARY AMOUNTS	UNIT PRICE AMOUNT PAID
D	DATE	ACTUAL CALENDAR DATE	DATE ORDER PLACED PROMISED DELIVERY DATE
T	TEXT	DATA HAVING RELATIVELY UNDEFINED CONTENT.	ITEM DESCRIPTION SHIPPING INSTRUCTIONS
F	FLAG	A CODE EXPRESSED AS A BIT AND LIMITED TO TWO CONDITIONS.	DELETED RECORD FLAG
X	CONTROL	INFORMATION USED FOR CONTROL OF OTHER INFORMATION DURING PROCESSING.	CARD CODE TRANSACTION CODE
K	CONSTANT	DATA WHICH DOES NOT CHANGE VALUE FROM ONE TRANSACTION TO ANOTHER	COLUMN HEADINGS PRINT MASKS
%	PERCENT	RATIOS BETWEEN OTHER DATA VALUES EXPRESSED AS A PERCENTAGE.	PERCENT OF SHIPMENTS ON TIME, PERCENT OF SHIPMENTS LATE

Fig. 3-7 IBM "OF" language class words. (*Reprinted by permission from DB/DC Data Dictionary, #G320-6017. © July 1978 by International Business Machines Corporation.*)

abbreviations? In this section, we will discuss this problem and an automated solution to this problem.

Traditionally, standard abbreviation lists have been developed within an organization in a piecemeal fashion, one application at a time. The scenario that follows describes a typical piecemeal development of standard abbreviations. Let us assume that an organization has recently instituted a DA function. It has been decided that all new applications from this point on must adhere to the DA naming standards. Let us assume that the new payroll system is the first project developed after this point. As data elements are created during this project, standard abbreviations and prime words are developed to complement these data elements. These abbreviations and prime words are reviewed and approved by both the data processing development staff and the payroll department end users. After nine months, the payroll project is completed, and the new payroll system is implemented into production. Let us assume that the next development project is the new personnel system. As data elements are created during this project, standard abbreviations and prime words are again developed to complement the personnel data elements. However, many of the prime words and standard abbreviations required by the new personnel system were previously created during the development of the new payroll system. In many instances, there is a conflict between the standard abbreviations created and approved by the payroll department, and those requested by the personnel department. For example, the payroll department created the standard abbreviation EMPL for EMPLOYEE. However, the personnel department has always used EMP to abbreviate EMPLOYEE.

As the above scenario illustrates, there are two basic problems with developing standard abbreviations and prime words in a piecemeal fashion. The first problem is that the first few projects developed only capture a small percentage of the entities needed for the entire organization. The second problem is that this piecemeal process is a very undemocratic one. Standard abbreviation and prime words should be defined according to popularity of use throughout the entire organization. For example, if the payroll department recognized EMPL as their abbreviation for EMPLOYEE, but the personnel, training, retirement, credit union, and accounting departments used EMP as the abbreviation for EMPLOYEE, then EMP should be established by DA as the corporate standard abbreviation. It is therefore important that DA collect as many standard abbreviations and prime words as possible and get approval for these throughout the organization as soon as possible. How can DA develop a comprehensive list as expeditiously as possible?

Most prime words and the words that can be used to produce standard abbreviations for an entire organization already exist in the data names

Full word	Abbrev.	Full word	Abbrev.
1. ABORT	ABRT	35. NAMES	NMS
2. ACCEPTABLE	ACCPTBL	36. NBR	NBR
3. AMOUNT	AMNT	37. NEW	NW
4. AUDIT	ADT	38. NUMBER	NMBR
5. BEG	BG	39. OUT	OT
6. CHAR	CHR	40. OUTPUT	OTPT
7. CHARACTER	CHRCTR	41. PARAMETER	PRMTR
8. CHARS	CHRS	42. PARAMETERS	PRMTRS
9. CHECK	CHCK	43. PARM	PRM
10. CLASS	CLSS	44. PGM	PGM
11. CODE	CD	45. POS	PS
12. COND	CND	46. POSITION	PSTN
13. CONSTANT	CNSTNT	47. PREFIX	PRFX
14. DATE	DT	48. PRIME	PRM
15. ENTRY	ENTRY	49. PRINT	PRNT
16. ERROR	ERRR	50. PROGRAM	PRGRM
17. EXEC	EXC	51. REC	RC
18. FILE	FL	52. RECORD	RCRD
19. FILLER	FLLR	53. REDF	RDF
20. FLAG	FLG	54. REJECT	RJCT
21. HEADER	HDR	55. REPORT	RPRT
22. HOLD	HLD	56. RPT	RPT
23. ILLEGAL	ILLGL	57. STATISTICS	STTSTCS
24. IN	IN	58. SUBSTITUTION	SBSTTTN
25. INFO	INF	59. SUFFIX	SFFX
26. INPUT	INPT	60. SYS	SYS
27. LAST	LST	61. SYSTEM	SYSTM
28. LENGTH	LNGTH	62. TABLE	TBL
29. LINE	LN	63. TBL	TBL
30. LIST	LST	64. UNACCEPTABLE	UNCCPTBL
31. MAX	MX	65. WORD	WRD
32. MESSAGE	MSSG	66. WORDS	WRDS
33. MIN	MN	67. ZERO	ZR
34. NAME	NM		

Fig. 3-8 Sample printout of automated standard abbreviation generator.

within the program source code libraries for an organization. Data Administration, Inc., has utility software available to extract all of the nonduplicate words in all of the data names from entire COBOL source code libraries. These words will then be listed alphabetically, and possible standard abbreviations for these words will be produced automatically. This comprehensive list can also be used to identify synonyms and prime words.

After preliminary review and modification of the list by data administration, this comprehensive list can be distributed for review and approval throughout the entire organization. By using software to automatically produce standard abbreviations and prime words, DA can assure thorough approval and compliance with naming standards. Figure 3-8 is a sample printout of an automated standard abbreviation generator available from Data Administration, Inc. The input to this utility can be:

1. Entire source code libraries (PANVALET, LIBRARIAN, etc.)

2. Individual programs
3. Individual record or segment definitions (e.g., COPYLIB)

Alias Standards

1. Aliases should only be used when identifying entities that occur in more than one programming language. Aliases are also necessary to link data names between proprietary and nonproprietary software. Unfortunately, existing software is likely to be full of aliases which cannot be easily removed. All other aliases should be prohibited by DA.
2. The alias name of a data element should be unique for each alias language type.

   Example: Data element: EMPLOYEE-NUMBER
   COBOL alias: EMP-NUMBER
   MARK IV alias: EMPNBR

3. No alias name should exceed the length allowed by the data dictionary or software language.

   Example:

Language	*Maximum length*
COBOL	30
FOCUS	12
MARK IV	8

4. The data element name must not be a reserved name within the target programming language. Below is an example of some COBOL reserved names.

   Example: CURRENT-DATE
   DB-DATA-NAME
   DAY-OF-WEEK
   RECORD-NAME
   RETURN-CODE

Version Standards

Sometimes it is difficult to distinguish between data elements that appear to be very similar in purpose. There is a fine line between two different data elements (therefore, two different data element names) and two versions of the same data element.

Normally, a VERSION of a data element is an entity that has the same purpose as another data element, but has different attributes. However, we must closely examine the attribute differences before we can determine whether to create a separate data element or a different version of the same data element.

Example: EMP-LAST-NAME PIC X(14).
EMPLOYEE-LAST-NM PIC X(12).

Since both data elements have the same purpose or definition, our first inclination would be to assign the same data name to both and create two versions (as below).

EMP-LAST-NAME	VERSION #1	PIC X(14).
	VERSION #2	PIC X(12).

However, depending on the length of an employee's last name, these two data elements may or may not be equal.

Example 1:

Data element name	*Length*	*Value*
EMP-LAST-NAME	X(14)	/S/M/I/T/H/ / / / / / / / / /
EMPLOYEE-LAST-NM	X(12)	/S/M/I/T/H/ / / / / / / /

Here, EMP-LAST-NAME *equals* EMPLOYEE-LAST-NM.

Example 2:

Data element name	*Length*	*Value*
EMP-LAST-NAME	X(14)	/C/H/R/I/S/T/O/P/H/E/R/S/O/N/
EMPLOYEE-LAST-NM	X(12)	/C/H/R/I/S/T/O/P/H/E/R/S/

Here, EMP-LAST-NAME *does not equal* EMPLOYEE-LAST-NM, and as a result, we should create two separate data elements:

EMP-LAST-NAME PIC X(14).
EMP-LAST-NAME-TRUNC PIC X(12).

(This situation should only occur in a retrofit environment. For new development work, only one data element should be permitted).

Below, is an example of two entities that have different lengths and formats but are versions of one another, not different data elements.

Example:

Data element name	*Format*	*Value*
STATE-TAX-ADDL-DOLLARS (#1)	S9(5)V99 COMP-3	/00/91/40/5C
STATE-TAX-ADDL-DOLLARS (#2)	999V99	/F9/F1/F4/F0/F5

Different group items may contain the same components but in fact be different elements, not versions of one another.

Example:

Data element name	*Format*	*Value*
ACTIVE-MIL-DUTY-END-DATE-1	MMDDYY	10/03/50
consists of:		
ACTIVE-MIL-DUTY-END-DATE-MO		
ACTIVE-MIL-DUTY-END-DATE-DA		
ACTIVE-MIL-DUTY-END-DATE-YR		
ACTIVE-MIL-DUTY-END-DATE-2	YYMMDD	50/10/30
consists of:		
ACTIVE-MIL-DUTY-END-DATE-YR		
ACTIVE-MIL-DUTY-END-DATE-MO		
ACTIVE-MIL-DUTY-END-DATE-DA		

To summarize, as a general rule, if two entities will *always* compare equally (regardless of content), then the two entities are versions of the same data element. When in doubt, create separate data elements.

Data Element Definition Standards

The definition of a data element should be clear and concise. Wherever possible, an example should be given to explain the purpose of an entity. The following rules should be helpful in developing meaningful entity definitions.

1. The definition of the data element being defined should not contain the data element name itself.

Data Element: BOND-DENOMINATION

Poor Definition: The denomination amount of the savings certificate at maturity.

Better Definition: The face value of the savings certificate at maturity. For example, the purchase price of a bond could be $50, and at maturity, this bond would be worth $100.

By using different terms in the definition of an entity, we provide the user with options in understanding the element being described. By doing so, we may be able to relate an unfamiliar term to a term that a user does understand.

2. The definition should describe the meaning and purpose of the data element being defined. The definition of a data element should not contain physical considerations related to existing data processing systems. While the physical constructs of an entity will change, the logical characteristics of a data element will probably never change.

Data Element: AUTOMOBILE

Poor Definition: Automobiles come from Detroit and Japan. Automobiles are Fords, Hondas, Chevrolets, . . .

Better Definition: Four-wheel vehicle designed for passenger transportation and commonly propelled by an internal-combustion engine.

Data Element: LOCATION-CODE

Poor Definition: Location codes are used in the ABC and XYZ files, and are used by the payroll, personnel, and general ledger systems.

Better Definition: A code used to define an organizational group, consisting of geographic region, division, area, and district.

3. For CODE-type data elements, when there are a limited number of values for the codes, the definition must include all of the permissible code values and an explanation of each value.

Data Element: US-POSTAL-STATE-CODE

Description: The standard alphabetic state abbreviation used by the U.S. Postal Service.

Note: These codes are used to validate the state in the vendor's mailing address. This alphabetic code is matched against the payroll system state numeric tax code in the Payroll System STATE-TABLE.

Valid Values: AK = Alaska
AL = Alabama
AR = Arkansas
CA = California
CO = Colorado
CT = Connecticut
DE = Delaware
DC = District of Columbia
FL = Florida
GA = Georgia
. .
. .
. .

4. For those CODE-type data elements, when there are a large number of different values for the codes, or if these values change frequently, the dictionary should not be used to document all possible CODE values. However, if this is the case, the dictionary must indicate where a list of these codes can be found.

Data Element: GL-ACCT-NBR-CODES

Description: A code used to identify company costs or charges by account category.

Note: Refer to general ledger master file for a list of all valid account numbers.

In general, the criteria for determining whether or not to document the values of CODES are:

1. Volume
2. Volatility

STANDARDS FOR THE EFFICIENT AND CONSISTENT USE OF DATA

The following sections introduce some basic principles concerning the efficient and consistent use of the data resource. Wherever possible, samples of data use in COBOL programs have been provided to illustrate these principles.

Data References

In a typical application system, many different data names are used to identify the same entity. Following is an illustration of some of the redundant references in a human resource system for the data element SOCIAL-SECURITY-NUMBER.

SOCIAL-SECURITY-NO
PAYROLL-NBR
SSN
SOC-SEC-NBR
EMPLOYEE-NUMBER
EMP-NO
EMPL-NO
SOC-SEC-NO
EMPL-NUMBER
SOC-SEC-NO-KEY

Several companies have undertaken projects to filter and load data from existing production systems into a data dictionary. These systems were developed with no consistency or standardization of data use. The objective of these projects was to document the data usage in these systems. To do so, it was necessary to identify all aliases, homonyms, and synonyms for each unique data entity. Below, are statistics from projects involving two medium-size systems.

	Total of COBOL data names	*Total of unique data entities*
Company 1	3800	150
Company 2	2500	130

These and other studies have revealed an almost constant 20:1 ratio between the number of data names and unique data entities in a single data processing system. In other words, on an average, we assign 20 different data names for each data element used in a data processing system.

At first glance, this 20:1 ratio appears to be too high. After all, many CODE-, FLAG-, or INDICATOR-type elements may only be referenced once (and thus given only one name) in a data processing system. However, more commonly used data elements may be assigned *several hundred* different names throughout a system. Below, are statistics from a project that identified all homonyms, synonyms, and aliases for the data element EMPLOYEE-NUMBER.

Number of programs in the system = 250

Number of lines of code = 1,000,000

Number of different COBOL data names = 6,000

Number of different COBOL data names for EMPLOYEE-NUMBER = 300

With a strong DA organization and the proper tools to check for redundancies we should be able to drastically reduce the number of data elements used in future data processing systems.

If we have historically assigned 20 different data names for each data element used in a system, theoretically we should be able to reduce the total number of data names used in a new system by 95 percent. However, in practice, we will be unable to achieve such a significant reduction for the following reasons:

1. Redundancy is not only a problem in our data processing systems, but is also ingrained in company policies from which these systems were derived. In large companies, there is a significant amount of overlap or duplication of effort. This creates the need for redundant data to support these duplicated company functions. To completely eliminate this redundancy would require major reorganization and policy changes throughout a company. This may never be achieved.
2. Even if we eliminate most redundancy in the data used in new systems, many of these systems must still interface with old systems. These old systems contain many data elements that are variations or versions of the data elements used in the new systems. We must therefore maintain some aliases in order to link the old and new systems. As old systems are gradually replaced with new systems, we can phase out these nonnormal data elements.
3. The use of proprietary software is increasing at a rate faster than the increase in "home-grown" systems. In other words, companies are increasing their use of purchased packages more than their use of software written in-house. When using packaged software, a company must maintain "company-brand" data names and proprietary software aliases for these names. The increased use of proprietary software tends to inflate the reference redundancy within our system.

Even after these factors have been taken into consideration, we can still realistically expect a 75 percent reduction in the number of data elements used in systems developed in-house. However, even a 75 percent reduction will result in significant savings in future maintenance costs for these systems. See Automated Redundancy Auditing Tools, in Chapter 4, for a detailed discussion of automated tools to detect data redundancy.

Data Attributes

The data administrator should advocate consistency in the characteristics of data. Regardless of where a data element is used, the length assigned to this data element should be consistent. For example, EMPLOYEE-LAST-NAME may have different sizes for different occurrences in a human resource system.

Example: EMPLOYEE-LAST-NAME PIC X(25)
PIC X(20)
PIC X(22)

The length of a data element should be assigned to maximize its use throughout an organization. When there is disagreement over the design of the length for a data element, opt for the maximum size. This will permit storage of any of the other variations in this standard data element. For example, the following data element name can accommodate any of the three variations described above.

EMPLOYEE-LAST-NAME PIC X(25).

Data administration should also encourage consistency of decimal alignment or precision of numeric fields. For example, the following PERCENT-type data elements lack consistency in their decimal alignment.

Example: SALARY-INCREASE-PERCENT PIC V99.
PERCENT-OF-MARKUP PIC V9999.
SALES-INCREASE-PCT PIC 9V99.

Consistency of the format of DATE fields is also important. Many of our systems use DATE-type data elements with a variety of different formats.

Example: LAST-POSTING-DATE YYMMDD.
EMPLOYEE-HIRE-DATE MMDDYY.
EMPLOYEE-BIRTH-DATE YYMMDD.

where Y = year
M = month
D = day

Since the format YYMMDD will allow a date field to be sorted in chronological sequence without shifting and without separate sorts for year, month, and day, this format is popular as a standard DATE format.

Consistency of format between the input, storage, and output uses of a data element is also important.

Example: SALARY-AMOUNT could be:

Input as 9(6)V99
Stored as 9(6)V99 COMP-3
Output as 9(6)V99

Does the savings in storage cost justify the need for an additional "stored-as" version for a data element? Wherever possible, maintain consistency of format for a data element regardless of where the data element is used.

It is sometimes impossible to avoid variations in the attributes for a given entity. The reasons for this are:

1. *Differences betweeen proprietary and nonproprietary software* If a data element must be passed between a software package and home-grown software, differences in attributes may be necessary to accommodate both systems.
2. *Differences between old and new systems* Rarely is a new system developed that does not have any links to existing systems. To be able to use a given data element in both an old and a new system, we must often create different formats for this data element.
3. *Differences in hardware* Occasionally, a data processing system may span different hardware. Therefore, the formats for the data elements used in a system must accommodate differences in hardware (e.g., word boundaries).

Data Groupings

As with data element redundancy, a poorly designed system increases group redundancy. Group redundancy occurs when a nonessential data name is created to identify one or more data elements. The following is an example of group redundancy.

```
00000100  01  EMPLOYEE-INFORMATION-RECORD.
00000200      05  EMP-ID-INFO.
00000300          10  SOCIAL-SECURITY-NUMBER     PIC 9(9).
00000400          10  COMPANY-CODE               PIC XX.
00000500      05  EMP-ADDRESS-INFO.
00000600          10  EMP-NAME.
00000700              15  EMP-FIRST-NAME         PIC X(14).
00000800              15  EMP-MIDDLE-INITIAL     PIC X.
00000900              15  EMP-LAST-NAME          PIC X(20).
00001000          10  EMP-ADDRESS.
00001100              15  EMP-STREET             PIC X(20).
00001200              15  EMP-CITY               PIC X(20).
00001300              15  EMP-STATE              PIC XX.
00001400              15  EMP-ZIP-CODE           PIC X(5).
00001500      05  EMPLOYEE-JOB-DATA.
00001600          10  JOB-CLASSIFICATION         PIC X.
00001700          10  LAST-10-RAISES.
00001800              15  RAISES                 PIC 9(5)V99.
00001900                  OCCURS 10 TIMES
00002000                  INDEXED BY RAISE-INDEX.
```

It is highly unlikely that the software using the above data will ever reference such group items as EMP-NAME or EMP-ADDRESS. It is unlikely that a source code instruction would be used to compare the entire contents of EMP-NAME or to move the entire contents of EMP-NAME. EMP-ADDRESS-INFO likewise serves no purpose, since it is merely a grouping of EMP-NAME and EMP-ADDRESS. The group name LAST-10-RAISES is also superfluous data, since it is unlikely that we would ever refer to all 10 table entries in one program instruction.

If the software will never use such data entities, why create them? Superfluous groups only add to the number of data entities in a system and increase the complexity of the data definition. Some will argue that the group name is needed to help document the purpose of the data elements within the group. If this is the case, then the names assigned to the data elements themselves probably are not meaningful enough. If further documentation is needed, a comment could be inserted into the data definition.

Let us recode the above data definition, and eliminate all unnecessary group entities.

```
00000100  01  EMPLOYEE-INFORMATION-RECORD.
00000200      05  SOCIAL-SECURITY-NUMBER       PIC 9(9).
00000300      05  COMPANY-CODE                 PIC XX.
00000400      05  EMP-FIRST-NAME               PIC X(14).
00000500      05  EMP-MIDDLE-INITIAL           PIC X.
00000600      05  EMP-LAST-NAME                PIC X(20).
00000700      05  EMP-STREET                   PIC X(20).
00000800      05  EMP-CITY                     PIC X(20).
00000900      05  EMP-STATE                    PIC XX.
00001000      05  EMP-ZIP-CODE                 PIC X(5).
00001100      05  JOB-CLASSIFICATION           PIC X.
00001200      05  RAISES                       PIC 9(5)V99.
00001300          OCCURS 10 TIMES
00001400          INDEXED BY RAISE-INDEX.
```

Comparing both examples, we have reduced the number of data elements by 33 percent.

$$\frac{\text{18 data elements} - \text{12 data elements}}{\text{18 total data elements}} = 33\%$$

We have also reduced the number of lines of code by 30 percent.

$$\frac{\text{20 lines of code} - \text{14 lines of code}}{\text{20 total lines of code}} = 30\%$$

Data Iterations

The first process in normalizing a data structure is to remove all repeating data groups. The following is an example of a data definition that contains repeating data groups.

```
05 PREVIOUS-3-SALARY-INCREASES.
   10 SALARY-INCREASE-1-AMOUNT     PIC 9(5)V99.
   10 SALARY-INCREASE-1-DATE       PIC 9(6).
   10 SALARY-INCREASE-2-AMOUNT     PIC 9(5)V99.
   10 SALARY-INCREASE-2-DATE       PIC 9(6).
   10 SALARY-INCREASE-3-AMOUNT     PIC 9(5)V99.
   10 SALARY-INCREASE-3-DATE       PIC 9(6).
```

There are two problems with this data definition.

1. It increases the number of data elements used in a system.
2. It is a very inflexible structure. If we want to store more than the last three iterations of salary information, we must create additional data elements and add those to the data definition. We must also reprogram each process that used this data structure.

If we are designing a database using the above data structure, we would decompose this data into separate segments. Each segment would contain one amount field and one date field. By doing so, we could add any number of additional amount and/or date segments without affecting the software.

If we are designing a sequential data structure (record or table) we could not physically separate the data. However, we can restructure the data to attempt to minimize further maintenance of this data. The following is an example of a more flexible data structure.

```
05 PREVIOUS-SALARY-INCREASES
   OCCURS 3 TIMES
   INDEXED BY INDEX-1.
   10 SALARY-INCREASE-AMOUNT     PIC 9(5)V99.
   10 SALARY-INCREASE-DATE       PIC 9(6).
```

Sometimes the occurrence of data iterations is more complex. Below is an example of data iterations used to store life insurance coverage amounts for persons of different age groups.

```
01 LIFE-INS-COVERAGES.
   05 LIFE-INS-COVERAGE-TO-65     PIC 9(6).
   05 LIFE-INS-COVERAGE-65-69     PIC 9(6).
```

```
    05  LIFE-INS-COVERAGE-70-74        PIC 9(6).
    05  LIFE-INS-COVERAGE-75-79        PIC 9(6).
    05  LIFE-INS-COVERAGE-80-84        PIC 9(6).
```

Since these data elements are used to identify both life insurance coverage amounts and age brackets, this is not a very flexible data structure.

Below is a suggested way to minimize data iterations and maximize flexibility.

```
01  LIFE-INS-COVERAGES.
    05  LIFE-INS-ENTRY
        OCCURS 5 TIMES
        INDEXED BY INDEX-2.
        10  LIFE-INS-COVERAGE-AMT      PIC 9(6).
        10  BEGINNING-AGE              PIC 99.
        10  ENDING-AGE                 PIC 99.
```

In summary:

1. Occurrence redundancy exists when repetitious data names are used to identify multiple sets of the same data entities.
2. If a data element name contains a numeric or alphabetic constant, it could be a candidate for occurrence redundancy.
3. Data iterations can be avoided in a database by applying the principle of first normal form. For an explanation for first normal form see How to Build a Normalized Data Structure, later in this chapter.
4. Data iterations in a nondatabase data structure can be minimized by tabularizing the data.

Data Coupling and Cohesion

To understand data coupling and cohesion, we must first understand process coupling and cohesion. The term *process* means something that acts upon data. A process is something that transforms, computes, or manipulates data. In physical terms, a process is a program, submodule, or subroutine.

Structured analysis and design methodologies advocate the design of data processing systems comprised of many small cohesive modules. A cohesive module is a process that has one and only one function. The purpose of a cohesive module can be described in one to two paragraphs of documentation. In terms of COBOL, a cohesive module is one whose Procedure Division normally consists of 100 or fewer lines of code.

There are several benefits of process cohesion. Process cohesion minimizes the coupling between programs. This simplifies the structure of the system and makes it easier to identify programs via their functions. This makes it easier to locate and modify specific functions within a system and thus reduces future program maintenance expenditures. Also, by minimizing program coupling, it is easy to reuse a given process elsewhere in a system. We can more easily clone cohesive programs from one system to another with minimal effort.

The same principle applies to data structures. We should create data structures based upon a series of simple, cohesive data elements. A cohesive data element has one and only one purpose. If the definition of a data element cannot be described in one or two simple sentences, then it is not a cohesive one. A cohesive data element minimizes the coupling between itself and other data elements. In a record or segment, there should be no linkage among nonkey data elements. Nonkey data elements should only be coupled with key data elements. This is identical to the principle of third normal form.

By maximizing data element cohesion and minimizing data element coupling, we design more modular, reusable, and portable data structures. The following is an example of data coupling and cohesion:

Data Element: VAC-PAY-YTD-HR-EMP

Description: The total annual or yearly vacation wages paid to an hourly employee.

Is this a cohesive data element? No. This data element not only contains an earning amount, but also describes the type of earning (VAC, or vacation).

If we decompose or modularize the data element VAC-PAY-YTD-HR-EMP, it becomes the following two data elements:

PAY-TYPE-CODE
PAY-YTD-HR-EMP

The definitions for these two data elements are as follows.

Data Element: PAY-TYPE-CODE

Description: A code which identifies the category of wages paid to an employee. Examples are regular pay, sick pay, vacation pay, overtime pay.

Data Element: PAY-YTD-HR-EMP
Description: The yearly or annual earning amount for an hourly employee. Refer to PAY-TYPE-CODE for a list of all possible earning codes.

Is PAY-YTD-HR-EMP a cohesive data element? No. This data element contains information about both an earning amount and the period of time when this amount was earned.

If we decompose or modularize the data element PAY-YTD-HR-EMP, it becomes the following two data elements:

TIME-PERIOD-CODE
PAY-HR-EMP

The definitions for these two data elements are as follows.

Data Element: TIME-PERIOD-CODE

Description: A code which indicates a time span.

Examples:

Weekly (week-to-date)	= WTD
Monthly (month-to-date)	= MTD
Quarterly (quarter-to-date)	= QTD
Annual (year-to-date)	= YTD

Data Element: PAY-HR-EMP

Description: The amount of wages paid to an hourly employee. PAY-TYPE-CODE identifies the type of wage this amount is for. TIME-PERIOD-CODE identifies the time span covered by this pay.

Is PAY-HR-EMP a cohesive data element? No. This data element contains information about both an earning amount (PAY) and the type of employee (HR, or hourly).

If we decompose the data element PAY-HR-EMP, it becomes the following two data elements:

PAY-AMOUNT
EMP-CLASSIFICATION-CODE

The definitions for these two data elements are as follows.

Data Element: PAY-AMOUNT

Description: The amount of wages paid to an employee. PAY-TYPE-CODE identifies the type of wage this amount is for. TIME-PERIOD-CODE identifies the time span covered by this pay.

Data Element: EMP-CLASSIFICATION-CODE

Description: Identifies the type of employee. Examples are hourly (H), salary exempt (E), and salary nonexempt (N).

In summary, the original data element VAC-PAY-YTD-HR-EMP has been decomposed or modularized into four data elements, as shown in Figure 3-9. Why is it advantageous to decompose VAC-PAY-YTD-HR-EMP and create four separate data elements? Below is a discussion of the benefits of designing cohesive data elements.

Reduction in Future Maintenance Costs Using the above example, let us assume that John Doe is an hourly employee and is being promoted (or reclassified) to a salaried employee. Thus, we must change John's classification (EMP-CLASSIFICATION-CODE) from H to E, but we must also zero out VAC-PAY-YTD-HR-EMP and move these wages to VAC-PAY-YTD-SAL-EMP. Thus, we must change the contents of three data elements. If we had created the following separate data elements:

PAY-TYPE-CODE
TIME-PERIOD-CODE
PAY-AMOUNT
EMP-CLASSIFICATION-CODE

we would only need to change the contents of one data element (EMP-CLASSIFICATION-CODE) from H to E.

The data element maintenance described above included changes in one type of earning (vacation). If Jane Doe had several different earnings (e.g., sick pay, holiday pay, jury duty pay, etc.) on her employee record, this maintenance effort would increase significantly. Thus, by designing data structures composed of cohesive data elements, we reduce the future maintenance cost of data processing systems.

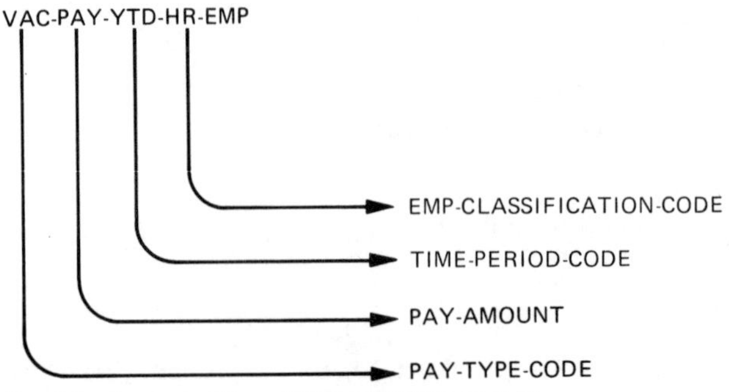

Fig. 3-9 Decomposition of VAC-PAY-YTD-HR-EMP.

Reduction in Total Number of Data Elements By designing highly cohesive data elements, we can significantly reduce the total number of data elements. Using the example data element (VAC-PAY-YTD-HR-EMP), let's demonstrate the difference in the total number of data elements based upon cohesive versus noncohesive data element design.

Noncohesive Using the noncohesive approach, we must create separate data elements for each combination of earning type and time period. Assuming that John Doe is an hourly employee, the following data elements would be required to store his necessary vacation pay information.

VAC-PAY-WTD-HR-EMP
VAC-PAY-MTD-HR-EMP
VAC-PAY-QTD-HR-EMP
VAC-PAY-YTD-HR-EMP

If John had a total of 20 different pay types, it would be necessary to create and define in the data dictionary a total of 80 different data elements.

Cohesive Using the cohesive data element design philosophy, we only need to design and document the following four data elements:

PAY-TYPE-CODE
TIME-PERIOD-CODE
PAY-AMOUNT
EMP-CLASSIFICATION-CODE

Thus the ratio between noncohesive and cohesive data elements is 80:4.

Increase in the "Span" or Usefulness of Data Elements The data element TIME-PERIOD-CODE is a highly cohesive, modular, and effective data element. As demonstrated earlier, by designing this data element, we were able to reduce the total number of noncohesive data elements in the payroll system by a factor of 20. However, the data element TIME-PERIOD-CODE can also be used by any other nonpayroll system or program that needs a data element to indicate a time span. Thus, by creating this cohesive data element and using it for all applicable programs and systems, there can be a significant reduction in the total number of data elements used in an organization.

Increase in the Modularity or Flexibility of the Data Design By designing a cohesive data element whose domain or role (values) can be codified, we are increasing the flexibility or modularity of the data element. For example, the data element PAY-TYPE-CODE could have the following values:

R = regular pay
S = sick pay
V = vacation pay
H = holiday pay

Let us assume that a company decided that employees are now eligible for pay while attending the funeral of a close member of the family. If we had not designed the data element PAY-TYPE-CODE, we would have had to create and document several new data elements to accommodate this change in company policy. By using PAY-TYPE-CODE, we only need to add an extra value or role to this data element: B = bereavement pay.

Definition Integrity

A data element should be designed for one, and only one, purpose. "Definition multiplicity" occurs when a data element is used for more than one purpose, thus the data element has multiple definitions. The following is an example of definition multiplicity.

Data Element: ALLOWANCE-CODE

Description: Two-digit numeric code. Indicates special groupings of employees and supplemental compensation payments.

1. Special groupings of employees.
14 = engineering union (ENG)
15 = executive payroll
16 = construction union employees (Texas and New Mexico)
19 = employee temporarily assigned to Phoenix from California

2. Supplemental compensation.
01 = None
20–79 = overseas service, flight pay area, hardship, rent allowance, per diem, and special compensation allowances.

The definition for the above data element is certainly not complete. Upon close examination, this data element is actually used for all of the following purposes:

1. Type of employee classification (executive or union)
2. The type of union the employee belongs to (engineering or construction)
3. Identifies the location of a union (Texas, New Mexico)
4. Identifies employees who are temporarily transferred
5. Identifies supplemental earnings eligibility

It is not difficult to understand why definition redundancy exists in older systems. They were often developed using fixed-length records. Their designers probably defined the original fixed-length records with plenty of extra FILLER characters for future expansion. Invariably, though, all of this FILLER was depleted as additional data elements were required to satisfy constantly expanding business requirements. After all available space was used up, the next new business requirement necessitated the expansion of the record size, and therefore a major modification was required for all processes that used this record. Instead, the additional business data requirement was often accommodated by expanding on the use of an existing data element. By creating this definitional multiplicity, a major change in the system was avoided.

Definition multiplicity is the single most serious infraction of the rule of prohibited data redundancy. It creates excessive linkage between data stores and processes and it certainly complicates the system design. Structured analysis and design principles encourage the engineering of simple, cohesive, single-function–single-purpose modules. The same concept applies to data. We should design data with a single definition and a single purpose.

Storage Redundancy

Storage redundancy occurs when the same data element is stored in more than one location. Storage redundancy is very common in some of our older systems. There was a tendency to store identical data in multiple locations rather than share the data from a common source. Storage redundancy resulted for several reasons:

1. Database software was not yet developed.
2. The majority of data files used fixed-length format and sequential access techniques. Thus, the more information you stored in any one place, the longer it took to access it. Therefore, there was a tendency to replicate small amounts of data among several different data structures.
3. Because of limited communication between various application development groups or poor documentation, we may not have been aware that the same data already existed.

4. Even if we knew the same data existed elsewhere, we resisted the extra effort required to link our programs to external data stores.
5. It was more efficient to access all required data from one file, rather than going to a common storage location.
6. We did not want to modify or improve the quality of another data store so that we could share it.

Of course, there are many instances when storage redundancy can be justified. Storage redundancy is often a necessity in distributed processing environments. Ease and speed of access in an online arrangement may also be a valid application of storage redundancy. However, unjustified data redundancy is a liability to any system. When a piece of data is located in more than one place, it creates the need for multiple update processes to this data, and we must develop safeguards to ensure that the data remains consistent throughout the system.

The benefits of minimizing storage redundancy can be illustrated by comparing our data resource to other natural resources. Those of us who are conservation-minded have always recognized the benefits of recycling our natural resources. Recycling not only improves the aesthetic beauty of our landscape, but also has significant economic benefits. A brewery can manufacture aluminum beer cans from old ones more cheaply than it can by mining the bauxite to manufacture new cans. A pulp plant can recycle old newspapers more cheaply than it can produce paper from trees. Why don't we apply the same principle to our data resource? Why don't we recycle data? Why don't we use the same data element in multiple processes so they can all share the same data resource? By doing so, we can eliminate multiple update and reconciliation processes between data stores. Thus, we can conserve the resources required to develop these update and reconciliation processes.

Some data dictionaries have features which can help in finding the various types of data redundancies that were discussed. However, no data dictionary, by itself, can eliminate data redundancy. In fact, a dictionary can accommodate data variations and duplication if the data administrator allows data element versions and aliases. Because the dictionary provides the tools to detect and publish inconsistencies in data use to a large audience, this in itself can help to reduce unnecessary data variations. By using our data more effectively, we can make our systems more compact, easier to maintain, and less expensive.

Resident versus Derivable Data

When designing data structures, we must strive to minimize the overlapping or duplication of purpose among different data entities. For example, there is duplication or redundancy between the two data elements BIRTH-DATE and CURRENT-DATE and the data element AGE. In other words, there is redundancy between BIRTH-DATE, CURRENT-DATE, and AGE because AGE is directly derivable from the other two data elements. Since AGE can be calculated as CURRENT-DATE minus BIRTH-DATE, AGE is referred to as a "derivable" data entity. When designing data structures, we must ask ourselves: Which data elements do we want to permanently store (on some magnetic medium) and which data elements can be derived (and therefore need *not* be permanently stored on magnetic media)? As a general rule, we should not permanently store data that can be calculated or derived from other data elements.

Using the above example, if we store both BIRTH-DATE and AGE in an employee database and we must modify BIRTH-DATE, we must also modify AGE. Thus, by not storing data that is derivable, we could eliminate some future maintenance to this data structure.

There are two advantages to calculating or deriving data:

1. We reduce storage costs.
2. We reduce future maintenance to duplicated or overlapping data elements.

The disadvantage of calculating or deriving data (rather than permanently storing data) is that we use additional machine processing time to derive the data each time we must access it. Depending upon the number of instructions involved in calculating one data element from another, this could have serious implications for certain online or minicomputer applications.

The decision to permanently store or derive data elements is based on a hardware versus software trade-off. The following questions must be answered:

- By always deriving data (and not permanently storing it) are we paying too great a penalty in machine performance?
- By permanently storing redundant or overlapping data elements, are we increasing future software maintenance costs if we need to make changes to redundant data?

Program Data Starvation

The key to understanding any concept is to provide an example of the practical application of that concept. In this section, we will first illustrate how the technique of "program data starvation" can improve the design of data. We will then provide a definition for this technique.

For the purpose of illustration, let us assume that a personnel system consists of only four modules. A description of the purpose or function of each module follows.

Module 1: This module computes the age of an employee. It computes age as equal to CURRENT-DATE minus BIRTH-DATE. This is used to prepare birthday cards that are mailed to the employees.

Input data elements	*Output data elements*
EMPLOYEE-NUMBER	EMPLOYEE-NUMBER
EMPLOYEE-NAME	EMPLOYEE-NAME
EMPLOYEE-ADDRESS	EMPLOYEE-ADDRESS
BIRTH-DATE	BIRTHDAY-DATE
	EMPLOYEE-AGE

Module 2: This module reads in employee union information and prints union member mailing lists for each of the 10 unions.

Input data elements	*Output data elements*
EMPLOYEE-NUMBER	EMPLOYEE-NAME
EMPLOYEE-NAME	EMPLOYEE-ADDRESS
EMPLOYEE-ADDRESS	UNION-CODE
UNION-CODE	

Module 3: This module prints a Equal Employment Opportunity Commission (EEOC) report that is mailed to the federal government.

Input data elements	*Output data elements*
EMPLOYEE-NUMBER	EMPLOYEE-NUMBER
EMPLOYEE-NAME	EMPLOYEE-NAME
SEX	SEX
MINORITY-CODE	MINORITY-CODE
	TOTAL-BY-SEX
	TOTAL-BY-MINORITY-CODE

Module 4: This module reads in an employee master file record and prints an employee profile report for the personnel department. This report contains all of the information about an employee—one employee per page.

Input data elements	*Output data elements*
EMPLOYEE-NUMBER	EMPLOYEE-NUMBER
EMPLOYEE-NAME	EMPLOYEE-NAME
EMPLOYEE-ADDRESS	EMPLOYEE-ADDRESS
BIRTH-DATE	BIRTH-DATE
HIRE-DATE	HIRE-DATE
CLASSIFICATION-CODE	CLASSIFICATION-CODE
UNION-CODE	UNION-CODE
NUMBER-OF-DEPENDENTS	NUMBER-OF-DEPENDENTS
SEX	SEX
YEARS-OF-EDUCATION	YEARS-OF-EDUCATION
EMERGENCY-NOTIFICATION-DATA	EMERGENCY-NOTIFICATION-DATA
BENEFICIARY-NAME	BENEFICIARY-NAME
RETIREMENT-DATE	RETIREMENT-DATE
MINORITY-CODE	MINORITY-CODE

We will now discuss two different methods of designing the input data to these four modules

Method 1: Since the information required by modules 1, 2, and 3 is contained in the input data flow for module 4, we could create one input data definition (on COPYLIB, PANVALET, LIBRARIAN, etc.). This single data definition could be used by all modules. In COBOL, this data definition would be as follows.

```
01  EMPL-PERSONNEL-DATA.
    05  EMPLOYEE-NUMBER                 PIC X(6).
    05  EMPLOYEE-NAME                   PIC X(30).
    05  EMPLOYEE-ADDRESS                PIC X(30).
    05  BIRTH-DATE                      PIC X(6).
    05  HIRE-DATE                       PIC X(6).
    05  CLASSIFICATION-CODE             PIC X.
    05  UNION-CODE                      PIC XX.
    05  NUMBER-OF-DEPENDENTS            PIC XX.
    05  SEX                             PIC X.
    05  YEARS-OF-EDUCATION              PIC XX.
    05  EMERGENCY-NOTIFICATION-DATA     PIC X(30).
    05  BENEFICIARY-NAME                PIC X(30).
    05  RETIREMENT-DATE                 PIC X(6).
    05  MINORITY-CODE                   PIC X.
```

The data flow diagram in Figure 3-10 illustrates this design.

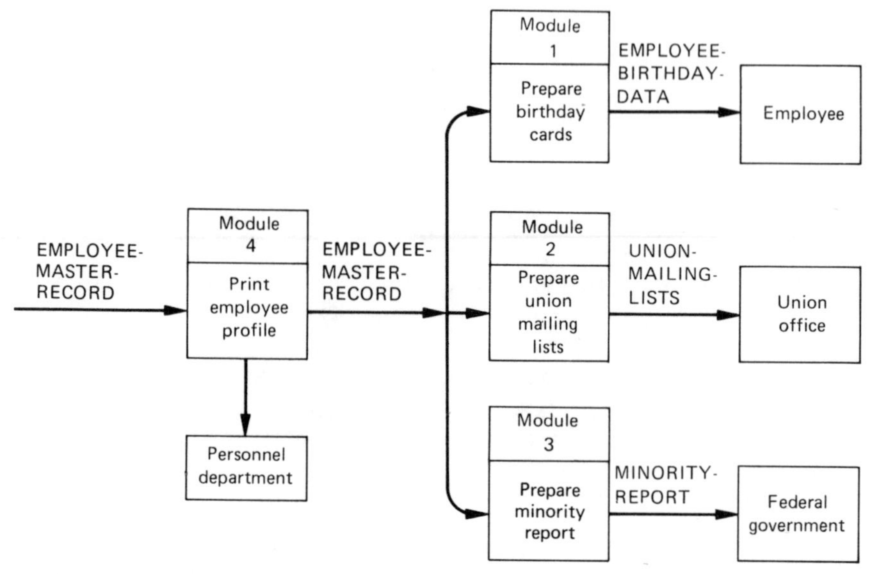

Fig. 3-10 Data design without program data starvation.

There are several disadvantages to method 1.

1. Since all four programs use the same input data definition, if a change is made to this definition, we must recompile all four programs.
2. Because the input data flow for all of these modules is EMPLOYEE-MASTER-RECORD, the data flow diagram gives us no clues as to the type of data that is actually used in which programs. Thus, the data flow diagram cannot help us understand the data usage in these programs.
3. Since all of the data elements in EMPLOYEE-MASTER-RECORD are available to all four programs, it is difficult to manage or control the data used by each program. For example, if a programmer decides to change a program to use additional data elements contained within EMPLOYEE-MASTER-RECORD, neither the data administrator nor the systems analyst will be aware of this design change. Thus, it is difficult to administer change control of the data usage in these programs.
4. It is difficult to analyze or map the data usage in this system. For example, suppose we must change UNION-CODE from a two-position field to a three-position field. By scanning the data dictionary or other system documentation, all we can ascertain is that UNION-CODE is contained in the data that is input to all four programs. We do not know which programs actually use UNION-CODE. Therefore, we cannot accurately estimate the costs to modify these programs if there is a change in the design of UNION-CODE.

Next, let's look at a better way to design the input data for these modules.

Method 2: Create a different input data definition for each program. In COBOL, these data definitions would be as follows.

```
01  EMPLOYEE-AGE-DATA.
    05  EMPLOYEE-NUMBER                      PIC X(6).
    05  EMPLOYEE-NAME                        PIC X(30).
    05  EMPLOYEE-ADDRESS                     PIC X(30).
    05  BIRTH-DATE                           PIC X(6).

01  EMPLOYEE-UNION-DATA.
    05  EMPLOYEE-NUMBER                      PIC X(6).
    05  EMPLOYEE-NAME                        PIC X(30).
    05  EMPLOYEE-ADDRESS                     PIC X(30).
    05  UNION-CODE                           PIC XX.
01  EMPLOYEE-MINORITY-DATA.
    05  EMPLOYEE-NUMBER                      PIC X(6).
    05  EMPLOYEE-NAME                        PIC X(30).
    05  SEX                                  PIC X.
    05  MINORITY-CODE                        PIC X.

01  EMPLOYEE-MASTER-RECORD.
    05  EMPLOYEE-NUMBER                      PIC X(6).
    05  EMPLOYEE-NAME                        PIC X(30).
    05  EMPLOYEE-ADDRESS                     PIC X(30).
    05  BIRTH-DATE                           PIC X(6).
    05  HIRE-DATE                            PIC X(6).
    05  CLASSIFICATION-CODE                  PIC X.
    05  UNION-CODE                           PIC XX.
    05  NUMBER-OF-DEPENDENTS                 PIC XX.
    05  SEX                                  PIC X.
    05  YEARS-OF-EDUCATION                   PIC XX.
    05  EMERGENCY-NOTIFICATION-DATA          PIC X(30).
    05  BENEFICIARY-NAME                     PIC X(30).
    05  RETIREMENT-DATE                      PIC X(6).
    05  MINORITY-CODE                        PIC X.
```

The data flow diagram in Figure 3-11 represents this design.

There are several advantages to Method 2.

1. Since each program uses a different input data definition, we are minimizing the possibility that a change in data design will affect more than one program. In other words, by minimizing the number

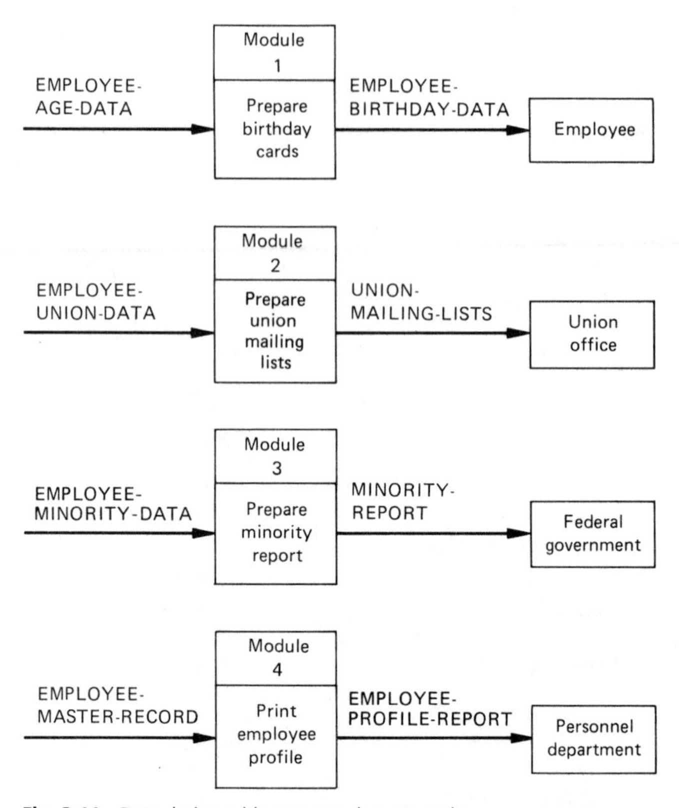

Fig. 3-11 Data design with program data starvation.

of data elements defined as input to each program, we are minimizing the overlap of data elements among several programs. This data design could reduce the costs of performing future maintenance to the programs using this data.

2. Since we have uniquely identified the data flows used as input to these programs, the data flow diagram provides better documentation about the function of each program. Since the input data flow more accurately names the data being fed to each program, the purpose or function of the program itself is more clear.

3. We are only supplying to a program those data elements that will actually be used by the process. If a change in the design of a program requires additional data elements, this change can only take place with the knowledge and consent of the data administrator. Thus, this data design facilitates tighter control over the data usage in each program.

4. It is easier to estimate the programming changes required as a result

of a change in data. Suppose the length of UNION-CODE is expanded from two to three positions. We know that UNION-CODE is only used by module 2. Therefore, we can more accurately estimate the costs to change this program because of a change in UNION-CODE.

The only disadvantage to method 2 is that we must create more data definitions than we need for method 1.

Method 2, above, illustrates the concept of *program data starvation.* That is, a program should only be provided with those data elements that it needs to perform its designed function. A program should be "starved" of the data that it does not use. If a program only needs three data elements to perform its function, then its input should consist of three, and only three, data elements.

Normalization Standards

When describing database structures, data administrators and database administrators tend to speak a language that is completely foreign to most data processing people. The following are examples of frequently used normalization terms:

- Third normal form
- Canonical synthesis
- Semantic disintegrity
- Transitive dependency
- Concatenated keys

The purpose of this section is to explain normalization as simply as possible. First we explain normalization and how an organization can benefit by using normalized data. Next, we provide step-by-step instructions for building a normalized data structure. A sample exercise in normalization techniques then follows. Finally, we introduce some normalization standards and point out some possible resistance to the implementation of these standards within an organization.

What is Normalization? *Normalization* is the process of developing a highly structured logical data design. The principle of normalization of data is very similar to the principle of structured process (or program) design. The objectives of normalization are:

1. Minimize the coupling between data
2. Maximize data cohesion

3. Minimize the storage of redundant information
4. Build a data structure that can be easily modified
5. Minimize the impact on the software that uses this data, if the data structure is modified
6. Build a logical data structure that is independent of the hardware and software used in the DBMS
7. Provide the database administrator with a foundation for building a physical database

The inputs to the normalization process are groups of data elements and the explicit or implicit relationships between these data elements. The output of the normalization process is groups of data elements (logical records or segments) that represent the purest and simplest structure of these data elements. In other words, normalization is the fragmenting and compartmentalizing of a complex data structure.

How Can Your Organization Benefit from Normalization?

1. *Meets end user needs* By using normalization, the design of the database is derived directly from the information requirements (user views). Herein lies its most important benefit. By using normalization techniques, we can assure ourselves that the data processing system being built will satisfy the end user's information needs.
2. *Flexibility* Those who believe in structured analysis and design of systems would think it foolish to design a physical processing system without first developing a logical model of the system. For the same reason, we should *never* design a physical database without first developing a logical database model. This is because a logical database design provides for a more flexible physical data structure.
3. *Lower future maintenance costs* If future business requirements necessitate a change to the structure of the database, we can minimize the cost of this change by designing a flexible physical database. This flexible database can only be accomplished by first building a well-designed logical data model.

   By building a modular data structure, we can also minimize future maintenance costs to the programs that use this data. Normalization techniques also minimize data redundancy. Thus, we can avoid multiple program updates to redundant or overlapping data.

4. *Faster application development* By minimizing redundancy, and maximizing the flexibility of updates and accesses to the data, we minimize the amount of programming required to maintain and extract the data. This reduces the process (or program) definitions necessary to use the database.

5. *Better understanding of the data* Many program design errors result from a lack of understanding of the data used in these programs. Before normalization can be exercised, the system designers must thoroughly understand the definition, characteristics, and relationships of each data element. By understanding the data thoroughly, many process design flaws can be avoided.

The data processing and user organization should contribute to, and review, the logical database design. They will gain a better understanding of the data used in a system and may be able to spot design deficiencies.

How to Build a Normalized Data Structure This section will provide you with a step-by-step procedure for constructing a normalized data structure.

Step 1: Collect all existing user views.

A *user view* is a collection of data elements that represents how a system appears to an end user. A user view is a particular external (rather than internal) aspect of a system. A user view is a system input or output medium. A user view is synonymous with an external data flow. A user view is a data flow from or to a source or sink. The following are examples of some common user views:

- Input form
- Hard-copy report
- Microfiche output
- Update screen
- Inquiry screen

Figure 3-12 is an example of a payroll summary report, or an output user view.

ACME PUBLISHING CO.
PAYROLL SUMMARY

AS OF 4/1/82

PAGE 1

EMPL NAME	EMPL CLASS	PAYROLL NO.	YTD GROSS	YTD TAXES	YTD DED	YTD NET
Abrams, John A.	H	83764	4,321.81	641.90	309.14	3,370.77
Charles, Robert B.	H	18962	8,511.62	3,101.60	411.52	4,998.50
Jones, Alma C.	H	41263	3,116.80	214.80	63.45	2,838.55
Smith, Peter C.	S	17496	14,105.60	2,180.64	1,161.90	10,763.06
Young, Paula L.	S	11994	9,108.43	1,416.80	143.91	7,547.72
TOTALS			39,164.26	7,555.74	2,089.92	29,518.60

Fig. 3-12 Sample output user view.

Step 2: Identify all data elements in each user view.

From Figure 3-12 we can identify the following data elements:

```
PAYROLL-SUMMARY-REPORT = EMPL-NAME
                         EMPL-CLASSIFICATION-CODE
                         EMPL-PAYROLL-NUMBER
                         EMPL-YTD-GROSS-WAGES
                         EMPL-YTD-TAXES
                         EMPL-YTD-DEDUCTIONS
                         EMPL-YTD-NET
                         COMPANY-TOTAL-YTD-GROSS-WAGES
                         COMPANY-TOTAL-YTD-TAXES
                         COMPANY-TOTAL-YTD-DEDUCTIONS
                         COMPANY-TOTAL-YTD-NET

EMPL-NAME = EMPL-LAST-NAME
            EMPL-FIRST-NAME
            EMPL-MIDDLE-INITIAL
```

Step 3: Define each data element, and store these definitions on the data dictionary.

Below are some sample data element definitions from this user view.

Data Element Name: EMPL-CLASSIFICATION-CODE

Definition: A category that identifies how the pay for an employee is calculated.

Valid Values: S = salaried employee
H = hourly employee

Data Element Name: COMPANY-TOTAL-YTD-NET

Definition: The annual or yearly total net earnings paid to all company employees as of the current payroll period.

Step 4: Identify and map the associations among all data elements in a given user view.

For example, what is the relationship between EMPL-NAME and EMPL-PAYROLL-NUMBER? EMPL-PAYROLL-NUMBER identifies EMPL-NAME. However,

EMPL-NAME could also identify EMPL-PAYROLL-NUMBER. We would represent this relationship as follows:

$$\text{EMPL-PAYROLL-NUMBER} \longrightarrow \text{EMPL-NAME}$$
$$\text{EMPL-NAME} \longrightarrow \text{EMPL-PAYROLL-NUMBER}$$

or

$$\text{EMPL-NAME} \longleftrightarrow \text{EMPL-PAYROLL-NUMBER}$$

This is an example of a one-to-one relationship. The following is an example of a one-to-many relationship.

$$\begin{array}{rl} \text{manager} \longrightarrow & \text{subordinate 1} \\ \longrightarrow & \text{subordinate 2} \\ \longrightarrow & \text{subordinate 3} \\ \vdots & \vdots \\ \longrightarrow & \text{subordinate N} \end{array}$$

We can represent this relationship with a double-headed arrow ($\twoheadrightarrow$). Thus, the relationship between manager and subordinates can be diagrammed as follows, since a manager could have several subordinates.

$$\text{manager} \twoheadrightarrow \text{subordinate}$$

The following is an example of a many-to-one relationship:

$$\text{child} \twoheadleftarrow \text{father}$$

since several children could have the same father.

The following shows a many-to-many relationship:

$$\text{project} \twoheadleftarrow\!\!\twoheadrightarrow \text{employee}$$

since an employee could be assigned to more than one project at the same time, or a given project could involve more than one employee, this is a many-to-many relationship.

Figure 3-13 is an example of a relationship map for a simple user view.

Step 5: From a single user view, derive first normal form.

A record or segment is in first normal form when it contains no repeating data groups. In other words, to place a data structure in first normal form, we must remove multiple occurrences of the same data elements.

Figure 3-14 is an example of a user view in a payroll system. The

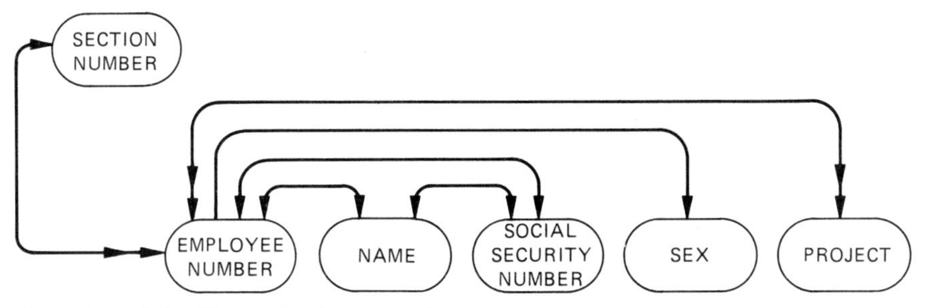

Fig. 3-13 Relationship map for simple user view.

diagram illustrates the association between an employee and the payroll earnings and deductions for this employee. In this example, both the earning amounts and the deduction amounts are repeating data groups, since the employee could have many different types of earnings and deductions in one paycheck.

We must decompose this user view by removing (or isolating) the repeating data groups. We do this by creating separate segments for each occurrence of earnings and deductions. The logical user view of Figure 3-14 should be compartmentalized as shown in Figure 3-15. If we need to include additional earnings or deductions for an employee, we simply add more segments. Likewise, to delete or inactivate an earning or deduction for an employee, we drop an entire segment. Thus, maintenance to these segments will not affect the rest of the data structure. This maintenance can also be accomplished with no impact on the programs that use this data structure (assuming that the programs were properly designed to handle any number of occurrences).

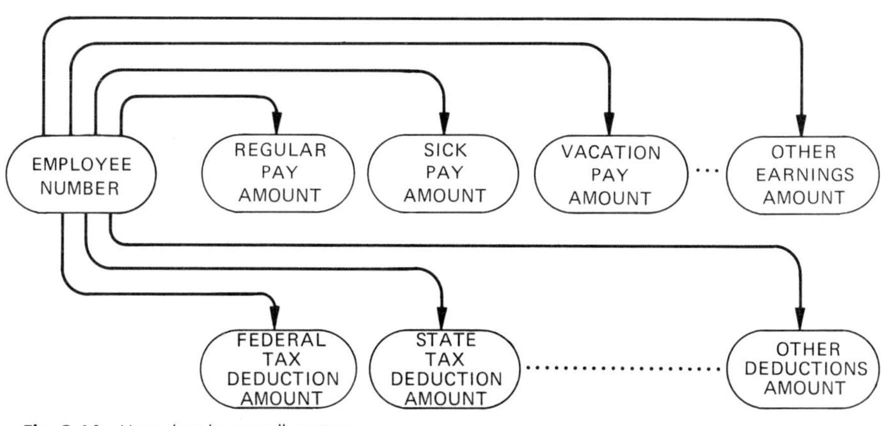

Fig. 3-14 User view in payroll system.

EMPLOYEE NUMBER	EARNING CODE	EARNING AMOUNT

EMPLOYEE NUMBER	DEDUCTION CODE	DEDUCTION AMOUNT

Fig. 3-15 Decomposition of payroll system user view.

Step 6: For each user view, derive second normal form.

A record or segment is in second normal form when all nonkey data elements are fully functionally dependent on the entire key. In other words, if any element can be accessed via a portion of the key (not the entire key), then the segment does not meet the requirements of second normal form. Figure 3-16 shows an example of a user view that is not in second normal form.

Key		Nonkey		
DEPARTMENT NUMBER	EMPLOYEE NUMBER	EMPLOYEE CLASSIFICATION CODE	EMPLOYEE SALARY AMOUNT	DEPARTMENT MANAGER NAME

Fig. 3-16 User view not in second normal form.

Figure 3-17 maps the associations between the data elements in Figure 3-16. This mapping between data elements illustrates that this data is not in second normal form. To access DEPARTMENT-MANAGER-NAME, we only need to know DEPARTMENT-NUMBER or the EMPLOYEE-NUMBER of the department manager. Thus, DEPARTMENT-MANAGER-NAME is not fully functionally dependent on the entire key (DEPARTMENT-NUMBER + EMPLOYEE-NUMBER). Likewise, we can access EMPLOYEE-SALARY-AMOUNT via the partial key EMPLOYEE-NUMBER (and do not need DEPARTMENT-NUMBER).

To place this user view into second normal form, we would decompose it into the segments shown in Figure 3-18. Thus, EMPLOYEE-CLASSIFICATION-

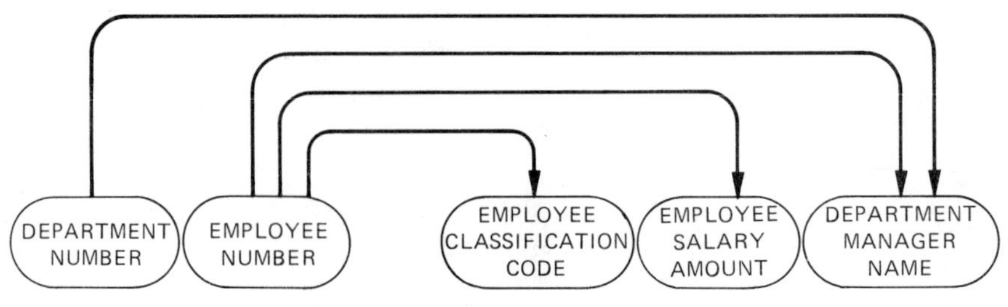

Fig. 3-17 Associations between data elements.

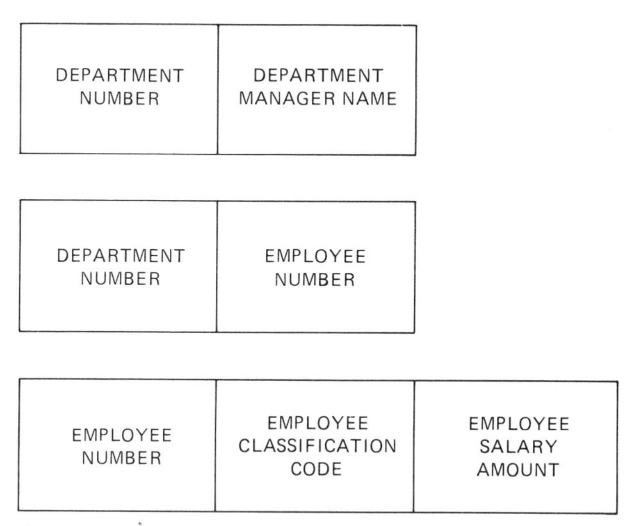

Fig. 3-18 Decomposition to achieve second normal form.

CODE and EMPLOYEE-SALARY-AMOUNT are fully functionally dependent on EMPLOYEE-NUMBER.

Step 7: For each user view, derive third normal form.

A record or segment is in third normal form when every nonkey data element is fully functionally dependent on the entire key, *and independent of other nonkey data elements.* In other words, a segment is in third normal form if it contains no transitive dependents.

Think of a transitive dependency as an intermediate key. If A identifies B, and B identifies C, then B is a transitive dependency between A and C. Figure 3-19 illustrates this principle. Figure 3-20 shows an example of a transitive dependency. EMPLOYEE-NUMBER can identify EMPLOYEE-NAME. SOCIAL-SECURITY-NUMBER can also be identified by EMPLOYEE-NUMBER, and EMPLOYEE-NAME can be identified by SOCIAL-SECURITY-NUMBER. Therefore, SOCIAL-SECURITY-NUMBER is a transitive dependency between EMPLOYEE-NUMBER and EMPLOYEE-NAME.

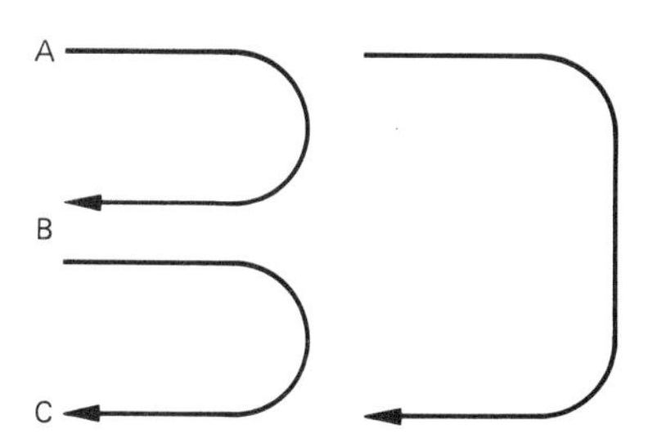

Fig. 3-19 Transitive dependency.

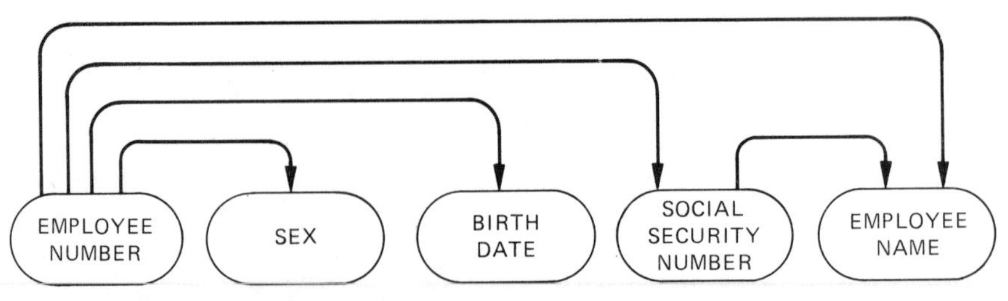

Fig. 3-20 Example of transitive dependency.

Transitive dependencies should be removed from this segment. Figure 3-21 below is an example of how to derive third normal form for this user view. By isolating the transitive dependency, we have eliminated all relationships among nonkey data elements. Thus, the data structure in Figure 3-21 meets the requirements of third normal form.

Step 8: For each additional user view, repeat steps 5, 6, and 7. As each user view is normalized, combine this with the existing logical database structure, eliminating any data or relationship redundancy.

Step 9: Revisit each user view, and verify that the logical database design will support the requirements of all user views. Ask the following questions:

1. Will the logical database structure satisfy each of the user input and output requirements?

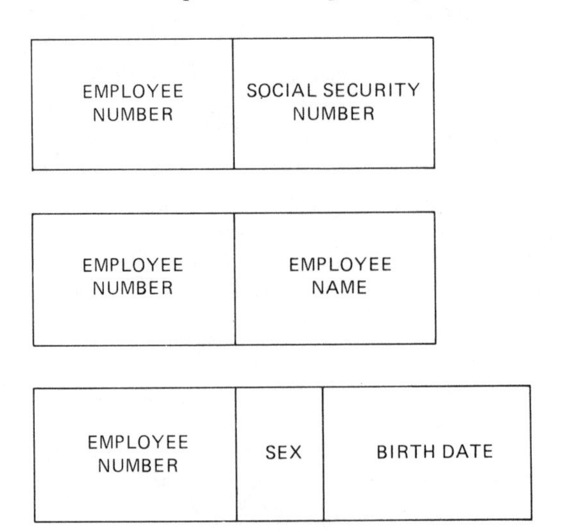

Fig. 3-21 Transitive dependencies removed.

2. Have we maintained all of the relationships of the original user views? If not, why not?

Step 10: Anticipate, and plan for, additional future information requirements from the database. Are there any other data access paths that may be required in the future? Will the users ever require other combinations of data that they do not now need? Besides existing user views, what other queries or searches of the database may be needed?

In summary, the steps below should be followed to develop a logical database design.

1. Collect all existing user views.
2. Identify all data elements in each user view.
3. Define each nonredundant data element, and store these definitions in the data dictionary.
4. Identify and map the associations among all data elements in a user view.
5. For each user view, derive first normal form.
6. Derive second normal form.
7. Derive third normal form.
8. Combine each normalized user view into the logical database design.
9. Repeat steps 5 thru 8 for each user view.
10. Once all user views have been combined into the logical database design, verify that this design will support the requirements of each user view.
11. Anticipate future user views and add these to the design.

Sample Problem In this section, we will demonstrate how normalization techniques are used to build a logical database design. Let us assume that the application development manager has been given the responsibility for building an online personnel system for the 100 employees of the Acme Manufacturing Co. This online system is to replace the existing batch personnel system. Sam Smith is the data administrator who provides data administration support for the applications development department. Sam Smith has the responsibility to design a logical database containing personnel information. This database must provide the personnel department with online update and inquiry capabilities for all employee personnel information.

The first thing Sam does is to collect all known input and output requirements (user views). They are listed here as identified by the users.

User View 1 (input): Since the personnel department only maintains a limited amount of information about an employee, they have requested that all new employee information be entered via one screen. Below are the data elements contained on this input screen.

EMPL-NUMBER	EMPL-SKILL-CODE
EMPL-NAME	EMPL-HIRE-DATE
EMPL-ADDRESS	EMPL-BIRTH-DATE
EMPL-SPOUSE-NAME	PROJECT-NUMBER
EMPL-CHILD-NAME	PROJECT-COMPLETION-DATE

User View 2 (output): For insurance purposes, the personnel department would like to be provided with a screen displaying the spouse and/or dependents for a given employee. Below are the data elements contained on this output screen.

EMPL-NUMBER
EMPL-NAME
EMPL-SPOUSE-NAME
EMPL-CHILD-NAME

User View 3 (output): When an employee terminates or is promoted, the personnel department must look for another employee within the company who could fill this vacant position. Therefore, the personnel department needs a screen that will list all employees who possess certain skill codes. If these skill codes satisfy the requirements of the vacant position, the manager would like to interview these employees. The following are the data elements that would be contained in this output screen.

EMPL-NUMBER
EMPL-NAME
EMPL-SKILL-CODE

User View 4 (output): Each week, the personnel department mails anniversary cards to those employees whose yearly company anniversaries will occur during the following week. Therefore, each week the personnel department will need a printout of all employees whose company anniversaries are approaching. Below are the data elements included in this report.

EMPL-NUMBER
EMPL-NAME
EMPL-ADDRESS
EMPL-YEARS-OF-SERVICE

The YEARS-OF-SERVICE for an employee is calculated by subtracting CURRENT-DATE from HIRE-DATE.

Next, Sam Smith, with assistance from the users, defines all the data elements in the data dictionary. During the analysis of data elements, it becomes obvious that YEARS-OF-SERVICE is a derivative of EMPL-HIRE-DATE and CURRENT-DATE. In other words, YEARS-OF-SERVICE can be calculated by subtracting CURRENT-DATE from EMPL-HIRE-DATE. Therefore, YEARS-OF-SERVICE will be defined in the data dictionary, but will not be stored in the employee database. Whenever the user requires YEARS-OF-SERVICE, it will be calculated and printed. The personnel department agrees with this.

Sam Smith maps the association between the data elements in user view 1.

EMPL-NUMBER ⟶ EMPL-NAME
⟶ EMPL-ADDRESS
⟶ EMPLOYEE-SPOUSE-NAME
↠ EMPLOYEE-CHILD-NAME
↠ EMPL-SKILL-CODE
⟶ EMPL-HIRE-DATE
⟶ EMPL-BIRTH-DATE
⟶ PROJECT-NUMBER
⟶ PROJECT-COMPLETION-DATE

Next, he identifies and removes any repeating data groups from user view 1. Since an employee could have more than one child or more than one skill code, Sam must remove these data elements and place them in separate segments.

Segment 1: EMPL-NUMBER ⟶ EMPL-NAME
⟶ EMPL-HOME-ADDRESS
⟶ EMPL-SPOUSE-NAME

⟶ EMPL-HIRE-DATE
⟶ EMPL-BIRTH-DATE
⟶ PROJECT-NUMBER
⟶ PROJECT-COMPLETION-DATE

Segment 2: EMPL-NUMBER ⟶ EMPL-SKILL-CODE

Segment 3: EMPL-NUMBER ⟶ EMPL-CHILD-NAME

By creating separate segments for each occurrence of skill code and children, Sam will be able to add or delete any number of these in the future without modifying the design of the data base or the programs that use the database. Thus, by creating separate segments, he increases the flexibility of the data structure. He also minimizes the future costs of modifying the data structure or the programs that update or access this data.

Next, Sam must be sure that all data elements within the segment are fully functionally dependent on EMPL-NUMBER and independent of each other.

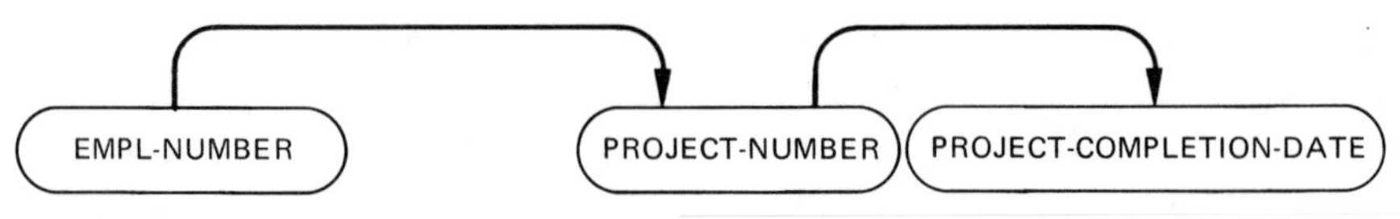

Fig. 3-22 Transitive dependency.

There is a transitive dependency in the above data structure. Since EMPL-NUMBER identifies PROJECT-NUMBER, and PROJECT-NUMBER identifies PROJECT-COMPLETION-DATE, PROJECT-NUMBER is a transitive dependency between EMPL-NUMBER and PROJECT-COMPLETION-DATE. Figure 3-22 illustrates this relationship. Sam therefore has to create a separate segment containing project-related information, as shown in Figure 3-23.

EMPL-NUMBER	PROJECT-NUMBER

PROJECT-NUMBER	PROJECT-COMPLETION-DATE

Fig. 3-23 Project-related information.

After normalizing user view 1, Sam arrives at the logical database structure shown in Figure 3-24. Will this logical data structure support user view 2? Yes. From the current date, a user can calculate the anniversary date for those employees eligible for an anniversary card

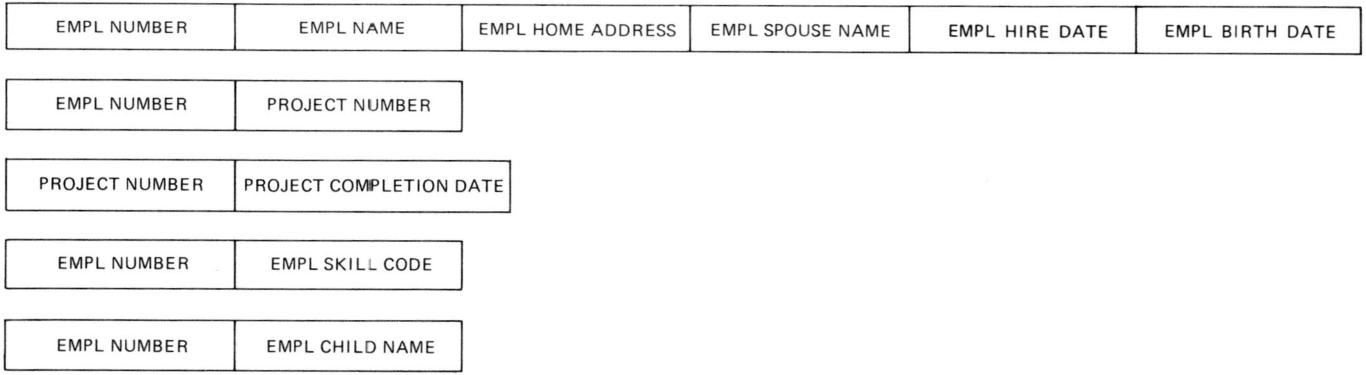

EMPL NUMBER	EMPL NAME	EMPL HOME ADDRESS	EMPL SPOUSE NAME	EMPL HIRE DATE	EMPL BIRTH DATE

EMPL NUMBER	PROJECT NUMBER

PROJECT NUMBER	PROJECT COMPLETION DATE

EMPL NUMBER	EMPL SKILL CODE

EMPL NUMBER	EMPL CHILD NAME

Fig. 3-24 Logical database structure for user view 1.

the following week. The user can then retrieve all names and addresses for employees whose anniversaries are upcoming.

Will this logical data structure support user view 3? Yes. Given a certain skill code, the user can find out all employee numbers associated with these skill codes and can then display all employee names for these employee numbers.

What about additional anticipated user views? Are there any additional user views that the personnel department may need? What if the personnel department needs information about an employee, but only knows the name of the employee? If this access requirement is necessary, another secondary index should be added to the design of this data structure. This secondary index would be as shown in Figure 3-25. By doing so, the user will be able to access employee information by using either the employee name or the employee number as a key.

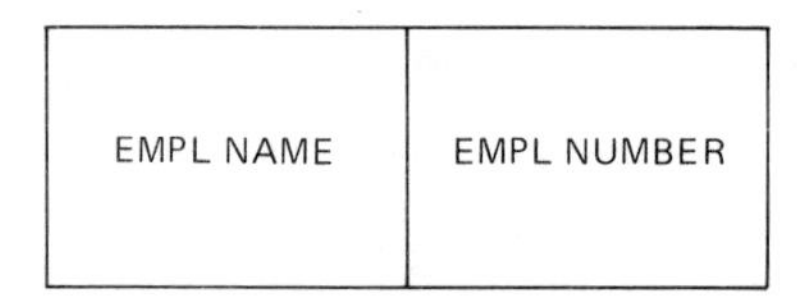

Fig. 3-25 Secondary index.

Since it is unlikely that a user will be able to anticipate all existing and future information needs, it is important that the data administrator help in anticipating all possible information needs. By building a data structure that can support as many user views as possible, we can assure ourselves that this logical design is the most stable one possible.

Normalization Standards for Your Organization Below are suggested rules that could be used as normalization standards for your enterprise.

1. No physical database will be designed without first creating a logical model for this database.
2. The logical database model must fulfill the requirements of third normal form. If the designer deviates from third normal form, these deviations should be documented and approved by the data administrator. Simply stated, a data structure must meet the following conditions:
   - There should be no repeating data groups within the same record or segment.
   - There should be no direct association between nonkey data elements. The only associations permitted should be between key and nonkey data elements.

- There should be no many-to-many relationships.
- A nonkey data element must be accessible only by means of the entire key.
- A nonkey data element cannot be accessible via another nonkey data element. In other words, there must be no transitive dependencies.

The above rules can be summarized as follows:

All nonkey data elements must be

> Dependent on the key,
> the *whole* key,
> and *nothing but* the key

3. Whenever possible, nondatabase data structures should comply with normalization requirements. To some degree, normalization techniques can be applied to any random-access data structure.
4. All data structure designs must have the approval of both data administration and the end user.

Objections to Normalization Occasionally, there is skepticism expressed concerning the hardware and other implications of using normalization techniques. This section will discuss some of the criticism or objections to designing a database using third normal form.

Concern 1: A normalized data structure contains more segments than a nonnormalized data structure. Does this increase the amount of storage used?

Probably not. This is because normalization techniques can greatly reduce the amount of data element or value redundancy between segments. A normalized data structure usually requires less storage space.

Concern 2: Because a normalized data structure contains more segments, aren't we using additional storage because of all the redundancy of keys?

Additional storage of keys may be required, but depending on the DBMS, these keys may only be disk addresses, and may not require duplication of all key data elements.

Concern 3: Because we are splitting the data structure into so many segments, or making it more modular, aren't we increasing the number of accesses to update or retrieve data? Won't this affect the response time?

Because normalization reduces value redundancy, updating a database usually requires less time than updating nonnormalized data structures. This is because we have minimized the need to access or update multiple segments for any given data element, or set of data elements.

Before normalization, the data elements necessary for one user view were entangled among many segments. After normalization, we have several small, cohesive segments that are independent of each other. Normalization does not necessarily cause more segment accesses or an increase in response time.

Concern 4 Why is logical database design necessary? Can't we skip the logical design process and begin the physical data base design immediately?

Unless we thoroughly understand the characteristics and relationships of the data, we cannot develop an efficient and flexible physical data structure. Without understanding the exact nature and purpose of each data element, we cannot eliminate data inconsistencies and redundancies. By performing this data analysis, we can reduce the number of errors encountered during the design and use of the physical database.

Concern 5 Normalization requires that considerable effort be devoted to data analysis and design. Doesn't normalization increase the elapsed time of the development of a system?

Normalization can significantly reduce the amount of value redundancy in a data structure. Normalization also provides for a more modular, flexible data design. This reduces the amount of process definition (programs) that is necessary to update and retrieve information from the database. Thus, normalization can actually decrease the elapsed time of system development.

DA Standards and the System Development Life Cycle Methodology

Incorporation of data administration could have a significant impact on the traditional process-driven system life cycle scenario. Adoption of DA standards, policies, and procedures could alter both the deliverables and the sequence of events in the traditional system development phases. The significance of this impact depends on the severity of the shift from a process-oriented approach to a data-oriented approach. The extent of change also depends upon the number and type of DA standards that are enacted in your organization.

The purpose of this section is not to provide a step-by-step procedure for implementing a data-driven design methodology. Several excellent books have already been published on this subject. We will however discuss the integration of DA with the system life cycle (SLC) process.

DA should strive to minimize the impact of data standards on the timely completion of the development project. It is our objective to improve the design of data used in a system, without sacrificing the success of the development of the system itself. It is important to detect violations in standards early enough to minimize the amount of redesign necessary to correct these violations. To do this, we must establish several DA checkpoints during the evolution of a data processing system. For DA standards to be effective, violations or standards must be detected as soon as possible after the violation has occurred. Unless violations of DA standards are uncovered and corrected soon after they occur, enforcement of these standards will be difficult (if not impossible). The earlier these violations are detected, the less impact they will have on the timetable for the completion of the project. The less impact this has on the delivery date of a system, the more support you will get from management in correcting violations to DA standards.

It is important that the data administrator document the interaction between the system development and data administration staff. The development staff must know what is expected of them, and when these deliverables are due. Table 3-6 contains suggested DA activities and deliverables during the life cycle of a development project.

It is difficult to ascertain exactly what impact DA standards could have on your traditional system development scenario. This depends upon the organizational structure of your company, the nature of the system being developed, the relationship between data processing and the end user, and the particular DA standards and system life cycle methodology of your enterprise. However, as a general rule, the more active participation you can receive from the end user and the data processing staff in the development of DA standards, the more effective these standards will be.

Table 3-6 Suggested DA Deliverables and Activities

Traditional development phase	*DA-related activities*	*DA deliverables*
1. Feasibility study	Define the entity class(es) that will be included in the scope of the project. Identify the subject data bases consistent with these entity classes. Map the associations among the project subject databases and the data structures of other subsystems that will be linked to them. Define the data flows and data stores that will, and will not, be within the scope of this project. In other words, define the data boundaries of the new system.	List and description of entity classes and subject databases. Maps or diagrams of the overall data architecture of the project.
2. Preliminary design	Define all pertinent existing user views. Define on the data dictionary all nonredundant data elements involved in these user views.	Data dictionary containing all data element names, attributes, validation rules, and meaningful definitions.
3. End of preliminary design	Define all anticipated user views. Identify the relationship among all data elements in each user view. Normalize each user view and integrate each user view into the logical database design.	Approved data dictionary. Approved logical database design.
4. Detail design	Develop the physical database(s) derived from the logical database model. Verify that the physical database design will satisfy user-view requirements. Define the groupings of all data elements involved in all system data structures (segments, records, files, tables).	Data dictionary containing all physical data flows and data stores used throughout the system.

Table 3-6 Suggested DA Deliverables and Activities (*Continued*)

Traditional development phase	*DA-related activities*	*DA deliverables*
5. End of detail design	From the data dictionary, generate all data definitions (e.g., COBOL FDs and 01s and database segments) to be used during the programming phase. Generate all data language definitions to be used by the DBMS.	Dictionary-generated source language data definitions on COPYLIB, PANVALET, LIBRARIAN, etc. Dictionary-generated data language definitions.
6. Programming phase	Make necessary adjustments to the programming language data definitions via the data dictionary. Upon the first clean compilation of a program, conduct program walkthroughs to assure that: **1.** All program data definitions were derived from the dictionary. **2.** Programmers have used data efficiently and consistently. **3.** Data manipulations and transformations agree with DA and programming standards.	Finalized source language data definition members. Program walkthrough approval.

Chapter 4

DATA ADMINISTRATION ACTIVITIES: WHY, WHAT, WHEN, AND HOW

In this chapter, we will discuss the cost effectiveness, or return on investment, of the various aspects of data administration. We will discuss the relative costs and paybacks associated with different DA activities. We will also provide suggested approaches and procedures to be followed to maximize the benefit from data administration. It is hoped that these suggestions will increase the profitability of DA within your organization.

ESTIMATING DA

Why Estimate?

As is the case with all resources, there is competition among many projects for the human resources of data administration. By estimating the DA-related costs and benefits of these projects, we can determine relative priorities for the use of these resources. In this way, we can establish a return on investment from the use of the DA resource. We can then develop a long-range plan for data administration based on the ranking of the costs and benefits of many proposed uses of the DA resource.

Because data administration is a relatively new discipline within data processing, there is a general lack of planning for the mission or direction of DA within an organization. There are also misconceptions about how the dictionary should be used to support the mission of DA. For these reasons, an organization may underestimate the cost of DA, or set unreasonable expectations from the efforts of DA. As with any other data processing project, DA projects should be estimated and budgeted before any effort is undertaken. By doing so, we can provide management with realistic goals and timetables for DA activities. This will improve the credibility of DA throughout an organization and improve the likelihood of the success of DA.

Estimating the Benefits of DA As previously stated, there are often several projects that are vying for the human resources of data administration. We must analyze the benefits of applying these DA resources to these competing projects. Although we cannot accurately quantify the tangible benefits of DA activities, it is important that we document the indirect or intangible benefits. Intangible benefits can be compared by assigning a relative weight (importance) to each benefit and comparing total quantities of intangible units among various projects. Although intangible benefits cannot be measured in absolute terms, they can be measured in relative terms.

There are many aspects, or responsibilities, of DA. We can compare these responsibilities by relating them in terms of the scope or dimension of each. In other words, DA activities can be ordered in terms of the span or breadth of these endeavors. For example, DA could undertake a project to develop a five-year plan for the implementation of new databases throughout the entire organization. Or DA could commit it to documenting all of the data elements within the purchase order database. Certainly, the span of the former project would be greater than that of the latter.

The relative operating ranges of various DA activities are illustrated in Table 4-1. These activities are ordered from top to bottom by the relative span or scope of each. These activities are also ranked by the relative impact DA will have in influencing the direction of your organization. In order to maximize the benefits obtained from the activities in the lower end of the hierarchy, we must implement these activities from top to bottom. For example, to minimize the redundancy and maximize the utility of a physical database, we must first plan and schedule the implementation of as many subject databases as possible. Without a top-to-bottom implementation of DA activities, the benefits gained from any one activity could be severely restricted.

Estimating the Costs of DA In the previous section, we discussed the relative benefits associated with various DA projects. We will now complement this with an analysis of the costs of DA activities. We will establish rules and guidelines for estimating DA tasks. We will then discuss some factors that can be used to prepare time estimates.

In this section, we will analyze several techniques to assist data administrators in evaluating the costs involved in various DA-related

Table 4-1 Relative Operation Range of DA Activities

Activity	*Scope*	*Sphere of influence*
Enterprise data modeling • Defining entity classes • Defining subject databases • Establishing plan for implementation of databases	All systems All data structures	Upper management
Data structure design • Logical database design • The design of other data structures • Advising/assisting/approving data structure design	One or more systems Databases Data stores	Data processing, database administration
Data entity design • Naming data entities • Defining data entities • Relating data entities	Individual programs Groups Entities	Programmers, systems analyst

activities. No attempt will be made to quantify these costs in terms of dollars, since this will vary considerably from one organization to the next. However, once you have estimated the time for each DA task, you can calculate costs by answering the following questions:

- What type of employee will be performing each task?
- Will any contractors or consultants be employed?
- What is the hourly wage for each employee type?
- Will fringe benefits or other overhead charges be included in this hourly wage?
- Will any work be performed on overtime?

General Principles for Estimating DA Costs The principles involved in estimating the costs of DA projects are similar to those used in estimating the costs of any data processing project:

1. Establish the overall objectives and scope of the project.
2. Break the project down into its component activities.
3. Estimate each activity.

In the following pages, we will discuss these principles in detail.

Defining the Overall Objectives and Scope of the Project Unless you document the overall objectives and boundaries of the project, you cannot isolate the activities that must be involved in this effort. Until you identify all activities, you cannot begin to estimate the total costs of these activities. The objectives and scope documentation must contain the answers to the following questions:

- What are the overall objectives of this undertaking?
- What are the DA deliverables to be produced?
- What are the boundaries or limitations of this effort? In other words, define what activities will *not* be included in the project.
- What will determine when the project is completed?

The following example illustrates the value of documenting the objectives and scope of a DA project.

Let us assume that your company has recently purchased an accounts payable software package. The software vendor did not supply a data dictionary with this package, nor does the documentation adequately define the data structures used in this system. Your manager has asked the data administration group to document the data usage within the software package.

The data administrator should immediately document his or her interpretation of this vague request. The documentation about objectives and scope for this project should contain the answers to the following questions:

- Is data administration to develop a data dictionary definition for every data element used in the software system?
- Is it necessary to document the data elements in the portions of the system that will not be implemented? Which programs or subsystems will not be used?
- What about duplicate or redundant data element names? How will these be documented? If duplicates exist, which one will be chosen as the primary name?
- Is DA to document the relationship between our company data elements and the software package data elements?
- Exactly what databases, files, records, or segments will be included in this documentation?
- Are you to document relations between key and nonkey data elements in these data structures?
- Is DA to combine these entities with the existing company data

dictionary or to create a separate dictionary for the entities within the proprietary software?

- Once this documentation has been established in the dictionary, should the accounts payable department manager and the data processing manager review and approve this documentation?
- Is the project completed when we receive sign-off on this documentation?

By answering these and other questions, the data administrator can create a foundation from which to estimate. Once the objectives and scope are defined, they must be reviewed and approved by your manager and all users of the deliverables from this project. Unless this process is followed, the results that management expects may vary considerably from what DA delivers.

Decomposing a DA Project It is impossible to establish a single dollar amount that will represent an accurate estimated cost of the entire project. It is necessary to break a project into as many small activities as can be defined. Only then can you accurately estimate the cost of each task. By totaling the cost estimates of each task, you can arrive at a more accurate total for the entire project.

How can all of the tasks involved in each DA project be identified? These tasks will vary considerably from one company to the next. These tasks will vary depending upon:

1. How DA is organized within your organization
2. The level of expertise of DA and other groups within company
3. The responsibilities of DA and other groups within company
4. The type of dictionary used
5. The DA standards and procedures implemented

These tasks will also vary from one project to the next within the same organization. However, there are certain tasks which are common to certain categories of DA projects. In this section, we will identify some common categories of DA projects and tasks that are typically included in these projects. These tasks are presented in the form of questions. By analyzing and answering these questions, you will be provided with a list of tasks that will be appropriate to the project within your organization. These questions may also provoke other questions that should be answered to successfully complete your project. These questions will also provide clues and stimulate ideas about how to estimate the costs for these tasks.

Category 1: Loading a data dictionary with information from an existing system.

Loading Information about Programs

- How many programs are included in this system?
- What type of program information do we want to document?
- Does this information now exist, or must it be created?
- If it now exists, on what medium is it stored?
- Can software be purchased or written to automatically extract this information and put it into the dictionary?
- What is the average amount of information (lines, pages, etc.) for a single program?
- How long would it take a data entry person to enter the information for one program?
- Who will review or verify the information after it is inputted?
- How long will it take someone to review the information about one program?
- What will be the dictionary reporting or search capabilities for program documentation?
- Do you want to link programs with modules and subroutines?
- How many links does an average program have?
- How long will it take to document this linkage for one program?
- Do you want to link programs with data sets, records, files, and databases? How?
- How many data structures are used by an average program?

Loading Information about Data

- How many data elements are to be loaded?
- How many synonyms are included in these data elements?
- How many data definitions (records, files, COPYLIB members, etc.) are to be loaded?
- How many data elements are included in an average data definition?
- Are software products available to estimate the volumes?
- Is DA to analyze and document where data elements are used?
- Is there software available to do this analysis?
- How long does it take to analyze, load, and verify one data element or one data definition?

Category 2: Creating data structures during the development of a new system.

- Is this new system a rewrite of an existing system?
- If so, how many unique data elements are in the existing system? Is this more or less than the number of data elements that will be used by the new system? Why?
- How long will it take to assign a generic name and a language alias for one data element?
- How long will it take to develop a definition for one element?
- How long will it take to enter the name and definition for one element?
- How long will it take to audit for a redundancy for one data element?
- How long will it take someone to review and approve a data element definition?
- What kind of reports will be created for data elements?
- How many data flows are involved in the design of this system?
- How long does it take to input one data flow?
- What type of application programming language or database language will the dictionary support in this project?
- How difficult is it to generate one data definition for these?

Category 3: Logical database design.

- How many user views have been identified?
- How many data elements are contained in these user views?
- How long does it take to normalize one user view?
- How long will it take to combine each user view into the logical database model?
- How long will it take to review one user view with the end user?

Category 4: Providing data dictionary training to the user.

- How much training material is provided by the vendor?
- How much additional training material is needed?
- How long will it take to develop this material?
- How many users must be trained?
- How user friendly is the dictionary?
- Will the user be permitted to make additions to, changes in, or deletions from the dictionary? If so, how many hours are necessary to train the user to do this?

- How many hours are necessary to train users to perform inquiries and create reports?
- How many hours of personal instruction must be devoted to each trainee during and following the training sessions?
- How many training hours are necessary for DA standards and procedures?

Helpful Hints to Estimating

1. Estimate your data administration activities from the past experience of other data administrators. Can other data administrators (within or outside a company) provide estimating advice? Have they been involved with projects that are similar to yours? Can the dictionary vendor provide any assistance or advice in estimating? Can they provide you with the names of other clients who have already performed work similar to yours? Do you participate in data dictionary or data administration user groups? Is DA estimating information available from the IBM GUIDE or SHARE groups?
2. Wherever possible, estimate large tasks by breaking them down into single units of work. Almost any project involves tasks which are repetitive in nature. For example, loading a data dictionary with the definitions of 100 data elements involves repeating the following tasks 100 times.
   - Research the definition.
   - Name the data element.
   - Check for synonyms.
   - Enter the definition.
   - Verify the accuracy of the definition.

   If, at the beginning of the project, you cannot accurately estimate the amount of time for one unit of work, start the effort anyway. Keep accurate records of the amount of time expended to complete one or more units. After a few units are completed, average the amount of time expended for one unit and extrapolate these hours by the total number of units involved.
3. Keep accurate records of all work expended in DA endeavors. At the completion of a project, analyze and compile a report of your experiences. These will prove invaluable in subsequent projects by yourself or other data administrators.

Limitations of Estimating DA Activities It is more difficult to estimate the DA workload involved in the development of a new system than it is to estimate DA workload in a system that has already been implemented. This is because the units of data and processes within an existing system are relatively static. In an existing system, we can determine the exact number of data elements, data sets, data definitions, and programs. In a new system, the number of data and process entities are continually changing. These entities evolve over the life of the system.

The accuracy of estimating DA activities in a new system is directly related to the maturity of the project. Has the preliminary design been completed? Have all of the data elements and data flows been identified? Have the processes been decomposed and packaged into programs? How many programs?

Estimating the workload involved in the design of data has some of the same restrictions as estimating the workload involved in the design of programs. Even if the number of primitive processes (or functions) involved in the design of the system has already been determined, the number of physical programs that will be derived from these processes cannot yet be accurately estimated. This depends on how these processes are packaged into programs. Likewise, even if the number of data stores in a system is known, it is difficult to estimate the number of records or segments that will be contained in these data stores. Even if the number of data flows has been determined, the number of data definitions necessary to support these data flows is not known. The number of data definitions depends on to what extent you modularize the data and also to what degree you practice data program starvation (see section Data Program Starvation, in Chapter 3).

To accurately estimate DA efforts during the design of a new system, it is necessary to qualify the input to these efforts. This input must be expressed as physical units of:

- Data elements
- Records
- Segments
- Files
- Databases
- User views
- Relations

However, we must also take into consideration the complexity of the data and the associations among the data elements. We must also consider the qualifications and experience of the data analyst performing these activities.

HOW SHOULD A DICTIONARY BE EMPLOYED?

In this section, we will discuss the utility and versatility of the data dictionary. We will also discuss the problems associated with this versatility.

The data dictionary is simply a database of information about data. In other words, it is a repository of metadata. The majority of these entities fall into two categories—process entities and data entities. Process entities include such items as systems, programs, modules, and submodules. Data entities include files, database schemas, subschemas, records, segments, groups, and data elements.

Some dictionaries even allow the end users to create their own entity types. For example, you could create entity types that are related to structured analysis and design. These entities could include data flows, data stores, and functional primitives. Thus, the number and variety of these entities is up to the imagination of the user.

Once metadata is loaded into a data dictionary, the dictionary can also serve as a directory for this data. In other words, dictionaries can be used to document the associations or relationships among entities. For example, the dictionary can be used to document the relationship between EMPLOYEE-NUMBER and SOCIAL-SECURITY-NUMBER. They can also be used to scan and identify associations among two or more entity types. For example, the data dictionary can be used to answer the following questions:

- What programs are in system *x*?
- What subroutines are called by program *x*?
- Subroutine *x* is called by which programs?
- Data element *x* is used in which records?
- Which programs use record *x*?
- What programs use COPYLIB member *x*?

Figure 4-1 illustrates some of the possible cross-referencing that can be accomplished by the data dictionary. The dictionary is also capable of linking, and documenting the linkage, between entities inside and outside the dictionary. For example, the dictionary can be used to generate programming language data definitions from entities within the dictionary. Figure 4-2 illustrates some of these capabilities. As we can see from the illustration, the dictionary can be used as a directory for documenting an enormous number of complex associations between entities.

Dictionaries can be used to store entities used in existing production systems and entities created during new application development. They

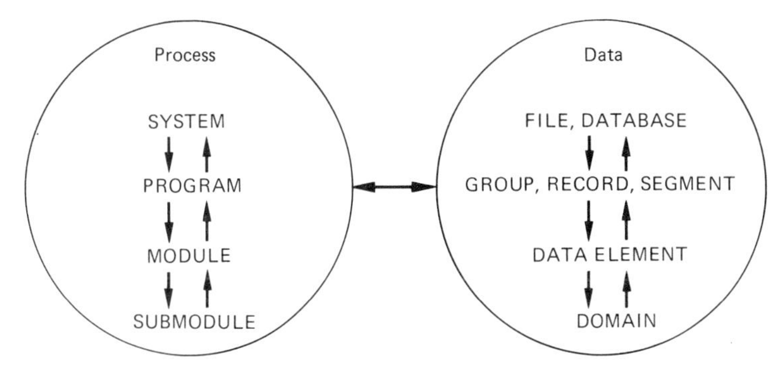

Fig. 4-1 Data dictionary cross-referencing possibilities.

can be used to store proprietary and nonproprietary entities. Dictionaries can also be used to document and control the procedures involved in the creation and evolution of these entities. For example, dictionaries can be used to record and monitor the events during the life cycle of a new application development. They are also used to manage the tasks involved in data modeling and logical database design. As we will discuss later in this chapter in Maintaining Control of Changes in a Dictionary, dictionaries can be effective in providing change control of entities.

Some of the data processing–related uses of the dictionary have just been discussed. What about its non-data processing uses? The data dictionary is not always used to store metadata. Sometimes it is used as a filing system for data itself. One installation uses a dictionary to contain customer name, address, and contract information. Other organizations use data dictionaries to document the standards, policies, and procedures for their companies.

We have just discussed the variety and versatility of uses of the data dictionary. It can be used as a filing and retrieval system for an almost unlimited variety of information. Herein lies the greatest pitfall of a dictionary. Although it can be used to store and reference almost any type of data, there are efficient and inefficient uses of the dictionary. If you cannot document the type of data to be loaded into the dictionary and what will be done with it once it is there, then the use of this tool has not been properly planned. Without the proper planning and control of this tool, it cannot be used effectively.

Although the dictionary is a central repository of metadata, this does not mean that *all* data should be stored there. If the data you want to load into the dictionary already exists in another medium, what improvements to the documentation or accessibility of this data will be gained by putting it in the dictionary? Is it possible to improve the accessibility and documentation of the data where it currently resides without putting it in the dictionary? How much will it cost to convert,

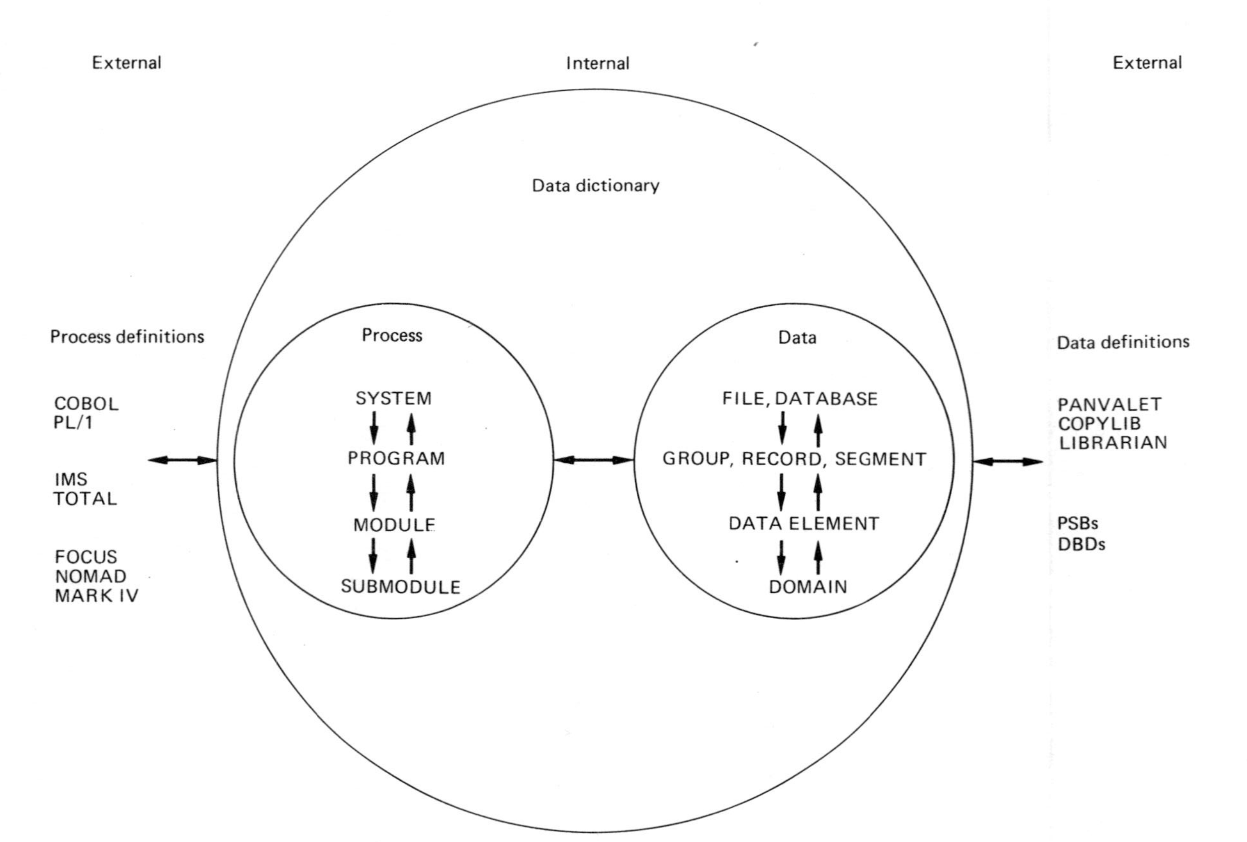

Fig. 4-2 Data dictionary linking capabilities.

load, and move this data to the dictionary? Is there any way to automate this process? Once it is in the dictionary, how must current methods of updating, accessing, and editing this data be modified? If some metadata is stored outside the dictionary, can this metadata be effectively linked to the metadata within the dictionary? Data dictionaries have certain limitations concerning the structure and organization of their contents, as do all databases. It is important to consider these before putting something in dictionary form. Which entities are and which are not most suitable to your dictionary? What are the access and update strengths and weaknesses of the dictionary? What cross-referencing or linking between entity types is possible with your dictionary? What are the search, query, and reporting capabilities of your data dictionary?

In summary, the data dictionary is a comprehensive, flexible tool for storing and accessing data. However, without the proper planning and control of this tool, little will be accomplished by its use. Putting information into a dictionary cannot be approached blindly or hastily. In this chapter, we will discuss the relative costs and benefits of the various uses of the dictionary.

HOW MANY DICTIONARIES?

When implementing a data administration function within an organization, the data administrator must address the following question: How many dictionaries should be developed to support the information resource management needs of the company? For a small company with only one location, the answer to this question is obvious. For a multinational corporation with several subsidiaries, the answer is not so apparent.

For large companies with several divisions or subsidiaries the number of data dictionaries implemented depends upon the commonality of data used by the various areas of the company. The data administrator must research the degree of commonality by answering questions such as the following:

- Which data elements or entity classes are common to the different areas of the company?
- What does the marketing division have in common with research and development?
- What data elements are shared by both the manufacturing division and the personnel department?
- What information is common to both the national and international corporate community?

Although multinational companies or conglomerates seem very disjoint, there is often a significant amount of data common to all areas of the company. Employee, budget, and accounting are examples of entity classes that are often shared by the entire corporation. For example, normally all subsidiary and divisional budgets are derived from a single corporate budget. Is the commonality of data based upon certain categories of entity classes? For example, are administrative entity classes (employee, accounting, etc.) common to the corporation, but product or service data elements unique to each division? Even if there are currently significant differences in data usage among the different areas of the company, are there future plans to being these differences into line with those of the home office? The answers to these and other questions will assist the data administrator in determining the number of dictionaries that should be implemented.

How many dictionaries are needed to serve end users in several remote locations? Even though a company may have divisions that are spread over a large geographic area, the information resource needs of this company could be satisfied with one central data dictionary. As Figure 4-3 indicates, the entire central dictionary, or segments of the dictionary, could be down-loaded or transmitted to remote locations. This will provide metadata and data definitions to a multitude of remote-site dictionary users. However, any updates or changes requested by the end users should be channeled through data administration.

How many dictionaries are needed to support the activities of several concurrent new development projects within the data processing department? Let us discuss the projects illustrated in Figure 4-3.

Project C has just begun. The analysts working on Project C have gained access to the corporate data dictionary to determine if it already contains any data entities that can be used during the development of their new system. No new entities have yet been created.

Project A is in the preliminary design phase. The team members have created several new data elements. These entities are contained within area 1 in the corporate data dictionary. These entities are classified under a "test" or "development" status and have not yet been formally approved by data administration. Although they are contained on the same corporate dictionary with other "production" elements, they are logically separated by their status.

Project B is nearing completion. The preliminary "test" data elements have been approved by data administration and have been changed to a "staging" or "preimplementation" status. Upon final approval from DA, these new entities will be changed to a "production" status, and will be merged with all other existing producting entities. Changes of status can only be initiated by data administration.

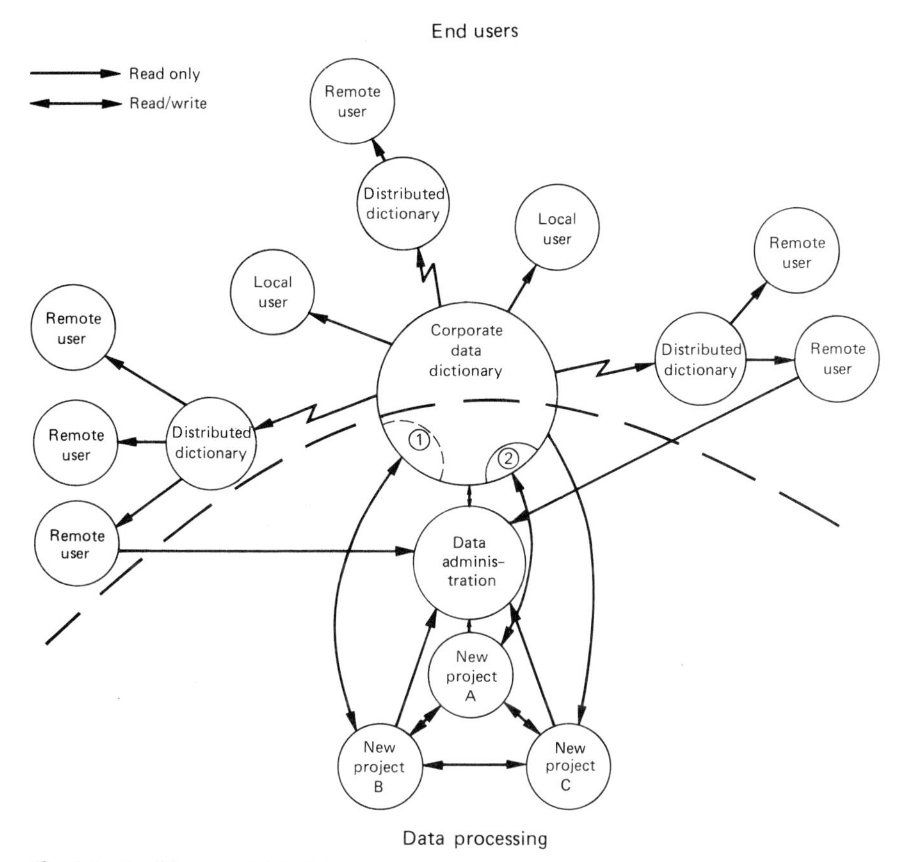

Fig. 4-3 Possible uses of data dictionary.

As illustrated in Figure 4-3, a single physical dictionary can accommodate the needs of several concurrent application development projects. Although these projects each have their own logical dictionaries, they are all contained within the same physical corporate dictionary.

MAINTENANCE OR NEW DEVELOPMENT?

As discussed at the beginning of this chapter, it is important to weigh the benefits of various DA activities to determine which project has the greatest payback to the organization. Should DA commit itself to assist in the development of the new general ledger system, or should DA become involved in the maintenance of the existing personnel system? In general, what is the relative payback of DA's involvement in new system development versus maintenance of an existing system? In other words, should DA and the data dictionary be used to document metadata

Table 4-2 Comparative Benefits of DA Activities

Maintenance	*New development*
• Provide documentation about the data used in existing systems	• Provide documentation about the data used in new systems • Improve the consistency and efficiency of data usage in new systems • Improve the flexibility and modularity of new data structures • Reduce data redundancy among new data entities • Increase data compatibility among data structures and programs

about existing systems or about new systems. Let us compare the benefits of each.

As Table 4-2 illustrates, there is greater potential benefit from DA's involvement in new system development than in existing system maintenance. This is because data administration standards and procedures cannot be easily applied to data usage in existing systems. Applying DA standards retroactively would require changing existing data structures and the programs that use them—an enormous expense. Therefore, little improvement can be made in data structures and data usage in systems already in production. However, in new system development, DA can actively contribute to the improvement in the design and usage of the new data structures. DA can assist and review data design to assure that it adheres to data administration standards.

What about those data processing shops that perform very little new development? In some data processing installations, maintenance of existing systems consumes 80 to 90 percent of the entire data processing budget. Thus, there is only limited opportunity for DA involvement in new system design. However, there is often new development work within system maintenance. While maintaining or enhancing existing systems, it is sometimes necessary to create new programs, reports, or files. It is within these activities that DA has the opportunity to implement rigorous standards for the improvement of data design and usage.

We have discussed the relative advantages of documenting metadata from existing systems as against new systems. What about the disadvantages of documenting metadata from existing systems? Most programming maintenance is applied to systems developed with little or no regard for standard policies and procedures for data usage. The data used in these systems will typically violate several DA standards. The data elements will probably have nonstandard names and attributes, will probably be duplicates or synonyms of several other data elements, and will probably be stored redundantly in several data stores throughout each system. To store such information in a dictionary could encourage and perpetuate its nonstandard use in other applications.

In summary, it is recommended that DA isolate itself from involvement with data usage in an existing system. Loading (or "retrofitting") a data dictionary with information from an existing system has little payback compared to the benefits gained from DA's involvement in new system design. Several software tools are available to analyze and document data usage in existing source code libraries without loading this information into a data dictionary. These tools can be used to create metadata on an as-needed or as-requested basis. Thus, these tools are capable of documenting data usage to support any existing system maintenance request, without needing to completely load all information about data in existing systems into a data dictionary.

THE USE OF THE DATA DICTIONARY: NEW SYSTEMS WITH OLD SYSTEMS

As discussed in the preceding section, the benefit gained from data administration's involvement in new systems development is greater than the payback received from putting metadata about existing systems into a dictionary. However, rarely is a new system developed that is independent of existing systems. More often than not, new systems are developed by gradually replacing or rewriting portions of existing systems. By doing so, systems can be implemented in phases or releases. By implementing a system in stages, the project development elapsed time and expenses can be more easily controlled. This also tends to minimize the training and conversion impact on end users.

Although there are several advantages to such an approach, phased system development presents a challenge to the data administrator. When dealing with such an environment, how can we maximize the benefit from data administration? At what point between the old and new system should you define the boundaries for the involvement of DA? How should DA define the scope of its data management efforts so that the size of the project will be manageable? Should metadata from both the new system and the old system be put into a dictionary? In this section, we will discuss these questions.

For the purposes of illustration, let us assume that the Acme Manufacturing Co. has decided to develop a new human resource system to replace its 20-year-old existing system. This existing system actually consists of three subsystems—personnel, payroll, and labor distribution. Because of the size and complexity of this system, it has been decided to implement the new system in stages. Since most maintenance problems occur in the payroll subsystem and the company anticipates major new federal government payroll-reporting requirements, the payroll subsystem will be replaced first.

Figure 4-4 is a data flow diagram representing the design of the new payroll system. E1 and E2 are programs in the existing personnel system that will feed data to the new payroll system. C1 and C2 are conversion programs that will convert the old personnel system data into a format acceptable to the new payroll system. Programs N1 thru N8 represent the new payroll system. Conversion programs C3 and C4 will convert the new payroll system records to the old labor distribution system formats.

Which data flows should be considered within the scope of data administration's involvement with the new payroll system? In other words, which data elements and data definitions should DA administer via the data dictionary? Since the data elements in these data flows were created during the design of the new system, they conform to the standards established by DA. You certainly want to document these data flows in the dictionary. The data flows marked with asterisks in Figure 4-4 are those that connect new programs with other new programs.

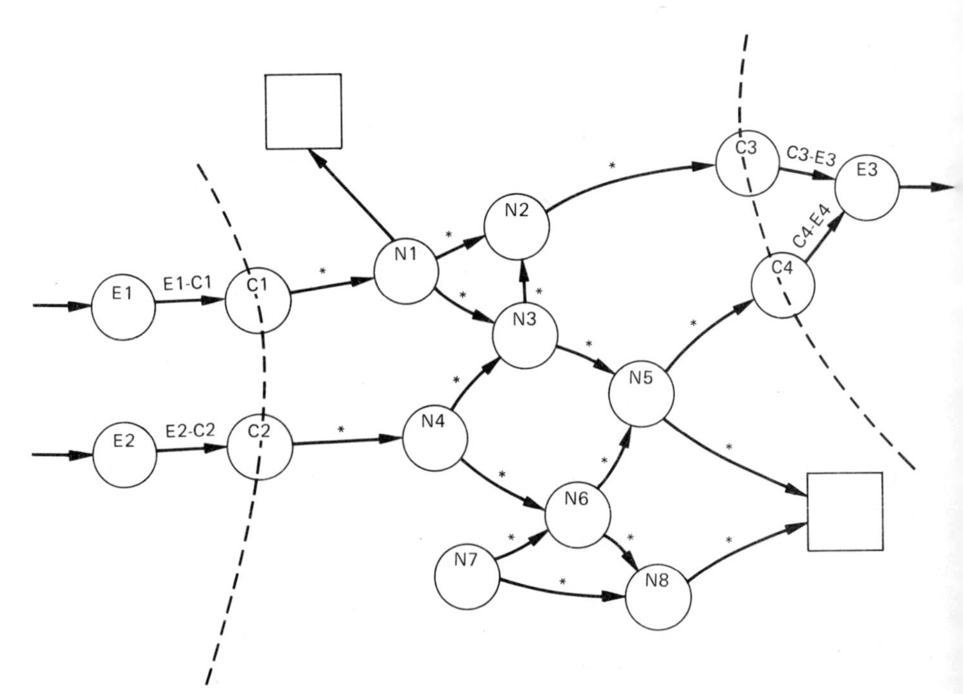

Fig. 4-4 Interaction of data dictionary with old and new systems.

What about the data elements and data definitions for the data passed between the new and old programs? Specifically, should DA concern itself with data flows E1-C1, E2-C2, C3-E3, and C4-E4? No, DA should not put the data elements in these data flows in the dictionary, nor should DA concern itself with generating the data definitions for these data flows from the dictionary. The reasons for this are as follows:

1. By reducing the size and complexity of the data management efforts, you are increasing your chances of success in the project. If additional time permits, you can later consider increasing the scope of the project to include portions of existing systems.
2. Most data elements used in the old system will not conform to DA standards. By putting these nonstandard "renegade" data elements on the dictionary, you are encouraging and perpetuating their use in other data definitions. By excluding them from the dictionary, you will help assure their demise.
3. In many instances, the data elements used in the old system will be variations or aliases of standard data elements used in the new system. The data elements below dramatize possible differences between these data elements.

	New system attributes	*Old system attributes*
EMPL-NAME	X(25)	X(18), X(20), X(24)
EMPL-WEEKLY-SALARY -AMOUNT	9(8)V99	9(6)V99 COMP-3, 9(6)V99, S9(7)V99.

   By defining these data elements in the dictionary, you significantly increase the total number of data element versions.
4. If you load these additional aliases and versions into the dictionary, you increase future data dictionary maintenance efforts. When you also rewrite the personnel and labor distribution subsystems, you should delete these nonstandard aliases and versions from the dictionary. How can you assure yourself that they will all be purged? What if other programs or applications have already started using these aliases and versions?

It is therefore recommended that DA's involvement in this project be limited to the middle area between the two dotted lines in Figure 4-4. What about the data definitions used by modules C1, C2, C3, and C4? Since the input to C1 and C2 involve the use of data elements from the old system, these should be excluded. Likewise, the output from C3 and C4 should be excluded. The output from C1 and C2 consist of data elements that comply with DA standards. Therefore, the data elements in the output from C1 and C2 should be included in the dictionary. The data definitions from these data flows should also be generated from the dictionary. Likewise, the input to C3 and C4 should be included within the scope of DA responsibilities for this project.

USING THE DATA DICTIONARY FOR PROPRIETARY AND NONPROPRIETARY SOFTWARE

Changes in the data elements and data structures of proprietary software should be made only when absolutely necessary. To do so could not only entail considerable expense but may also invalidate any maintenance agreement with the software vendor. There is therefore little that can be done to improve the design or use of data within proprietary software. For this reason, DA's involvement in software packages has many of the same considerations concerning maintenance of an existing system (see above, Maintenance or New Development?).

The data within proprietary software will not conform to your installation standards, nor will your data usage be consistent with that of the proprietary software. Likewise, no attempt should be made to modify the proprietary software's data design to match yours, or vice versa. Although your installation's DA standards cannot be applied retroactively to proprietary software, DA standards should apply to any future changes in proprietary data. Occasionally, a new data element or data structure may be added to the software package. When this occurs, the design of this new data should adhere to the DA standards of your installation. For example, if a proprietary database is modified to include a data entity that already exists within your organization, the name and attributes of this new data element should be identical to the existing data entity.

To minimize the potential incompatibilities of data between proprietary and nonproprietary software, data administration should be actively involved in the evaluation and selection of software packages. DA should be responsible for answering the following questions. Which vendor software (if any) provides a data dictionary as part of the package? Is all data used in the package extracted from a dictionary or central repository for data definitions (e.g., COPYLIB)? How consistently did the vendor assign names and attributes to data elements? Can the vendor supply the source code so DA can evaluate the consistency of data naming by running all of the proprietary data elements through a keyword list program? How modular or flexible are the data structures? Do the databases in the software package meet the requirements of third normal form?

THE DATA DICTIONARY: DATA VERSUS PROCESSES

As discussed at the beginning of the chapter, before any DA activity is begun, it is essential to perform a cost-benefit analysis of all projects competing for the resources of DA. The data administrator must also determine which DA activities are the most cost-effective dictionary applications. In other words, what types of information should, or should not, be loaded into the data dictionary?

Most information loaded into the dictionary can be classified as either process entities or data entities. Process metadata includes information about systems, programs, modules, and subroutines. Data metadata includes information about data elements, groups, records, segments, files, and databases. Which of these metadata types are the most cost-effective to document in the dictionary?

Data dictionaries are an excellent facility for storing the definitions and attributes of data elements. They are also very effective in documenting the relationships among data entities. For a large database, the dictionary is the only practical means to store and control the complex relationships among all data elements. Dictionaries are also very valuable tools for generating data definitions for records, files, and database segments. Therefore, the data dictionary should be used to store all data entities.

Dictionaries are also capable of storing documentation about systems and programs. For example, a dictionary could be used to store the program documentation for all programs in a system. However, there are distinct disadvantages to storing large amounts of text (e.g., program documentation) in the dictionary. The first disadvantage is that dictionaries have very little or no word-processing capabilities. If additions to, changes in, or deletions from the text of a dictionary must be done, it must be done on a line-by-line basis. That is, dictionaries will not automatically realign sentences and paragraphs to accommodate changes of words or sentences. The second disadvantage is that dictionaries are limited in their capabilities of handling upper and lower case letters. Dictionaries also do not have word-processing capabilities to scan, reformat, and make global changes in text. For these reasons, a thorough comparison should be made between the word-processing and data dictionary capabilities of an installation for storing textual information about process metadata.

Dictionaries are also capable of storing information about the linkages between process and data entities. A dictionary could be used to answer questions such as What programs use COPYLIB member X? and What programs use data element BUILDING-LOCATION-CODE? Some dictionaries are capable of dynamically generating this information each time a process is updated. For all other dictionaries, this relationship metadata must be loaded manually. However, there are two serious disadvantages to manually loading this type of information into a data dictionary. The first disadvantage is that loading this data is a time-consuming and expensive process. The second disadvantage is that controls must be instituted to update the documentation in the dictionary every time there is a change in the relationships between data and processes in the application programs and systems.

If you do not use the dictionary to document these linkages, how can these relationships be determined? There currently exist several automated tools to document the linkages between data and processes without loading this information into the data dictionary. These packages are capable of analyzing and synthesizing existing source code libraries to document the linkage between processes and data. This software can be used to answer "what if"-type questions including:

- Which programs use data element *x*?
- Which programs use record *x*?
- Which files are used by program *x*?
- Which programs are contained in system *x*?
- Which programs use COPYLIB member *x*?
- Which programs call subroutine *x*?
- Subroutine *x* is called by which programs?
- Which data elements does subroutine *x* use?

By using these software tools to analyze existing source code programs, the expense of loading and updating process documentation in the dictionary can be eliminated. These software tools will also assure that the metadata and the source code are consistent.

In summary, the data dictionary is the only feasible tool for storing large amounts of information about data. However, there are several disadvantages to storing process information in the dictionary. Also, unless process-data relationship metadata can be generated and updated automatically, it is recommended that this information not be stored in the dictionary.

How to Audit for Redundancy

In this section, we will discuss software tools and techniques to assist data administrators in the identification and elimination of redundant, duplicate, and overlapping data entities. We will discuss redundancy of data entities in terms of both existing systems and new systems design. For a more detailed explanation of automated redundancy auditing tools, see the section by that name, below.

Why Audit for Redundancy? As discussed in Data References, in Chapter 3, with proper data administration techniques, it is possible to significantly reduce the total number of data entities in an organization. By doing so, you can greatly reduce the size and complexity of the programs that manipulate these data entities and the cost of future maintenance of data and program structures.

Three Steps to Follow in Auditing for Redundancy There are three constructs associated with any data entity. These constructs are:

1. Name
2. Attributes
3. Definition

Each of these constructs can be interrogated when auditing for redundancy. These constructs are listed in the order with which the auditing should be performed. It is easier to detect duplicates by comparing data entity names than by comparing attributes. Likewise, it is less time-consuming to compare attributes than to compare definitions. Therefore, you should first compare names, then attributes, then definitions (if necessary).

Auditing Names Identifying similarities among the names of several data elements will assist you in identifying and eliminating synonyms, homonyms, and aliases. There are six factors that complicate a search for similarities in names:

1. The words of one data entity may be arranged differently than the words of a similar or duplicate entity.

   Example: EMPLOYEE-CITY-RESIDENCE-NAME
   EMPLOYEE-RESIDENCE-CITY-NAME

2. The name of one entity may contain more (or fewer) words than the name of another redundant entity.

   Example: DATE-OF-HIRE SOCIAL-SECURITY-NBR
   HIRE-DATE EMP-SOCIAL-SECURITY-NBR

3. One entity name may contain abbreviations of fully spelled words used in another name, or vice versa.

   Example: EMPLOYEE-HOME-ADDRESS COST-ACCOUNTING-CODE
   EMP-HOME-ADDR COST-ACCT-CD

4. The words of one entity may be synonyms of words in another duplicate entity.

Example:	EMP-TERMINATION-DATE	MONTHLY-PAY-AMOUNT
	EMP-SEPARATION-DATE	MONTHLY-WAGE-AMOUNT
	EMP-DEPARTURE-DATE	MONTHLY-EARNING-AMOUNT

5. The words of one entity may be spelling variations of the words in a redundant entity.

Example:	GEN-LEDGER-ACCOUNTING-DATE	LAST-ACCRUAL-PERIOD-CODE
	GEN-LEDGER-ACCOUNT-DATE	LAST-ACCRUE-PERIOD-CODE

This variation may be caused by the use of both the singular and plural spelling of the same word.

Example: EMP-HOURS-WORKED
EMP-HOUR-WORKED

or

TOTAL-BUDGET-WKS
TOTAL-BUDGET-WK

This variation may be due to different verb tenses used in different names.

Example: LAST-DAY-WORK
LAST-DAY-WORKED
LAST-DAY-WORKS

6. The name of one entity may contain an acronym for words in another similar entity.

Example:	HOURS-WORKED-YEAR-TO-DATE	CASH-ON-DELIVERY-AMOUNT
	HOURS-WORK-YTD	COD-AMOUNT

KEYWORD-IN-CONTEXT AND KEYWORD-OUT-OF-CONTEXT INDEXES *K*ey*w*ord-*i*n-*c*ontext (KWIC) and *k*ey*w*ord-*o*ut-of-*c*ontext (KWOC) indexes can be used to overcome some of the previously described difficulties in matching data element names. A *keyword* is a word that is used to identify, catalog, or label an entity, for example, the data element name EMP-HOME-ADDR contains the three keywords:

EMP
HOME
ADDR

These are referred to as *keywords in context* since these words are actually contained in the data element name itself.

However, there are other words that may be associated with the name EMP-HOME-ADDR. These words may be synonyms of the words used in EMP-HOME-ADDR. Such words are referred to as *keywords out of context:*

Example: EMP-HOME-ADDR

Keywords in context	*Keywords out of context*
EMP	ASSOCIATE
HOME	LIVE, LIVES, RESIDE, RESIDES, RESIDENCE
ADDR	LOCATION, STREET

We may also want to include abbreviations or fully spelled words in these keywords in context.

Example:

Keywords in context	*Keywords out of context*
EMP	ASSOC, EMPLOYEE
HOME	RES
ADDR	ADDRESS, LOC

The total number of KWIC and KWOC entries for EMP-HOME-ADDR would be as follows:

KWIC	*KWOC*
EMP	ASSOC, ASSOCIATE, EMPLOYEE
HOME	LIVE, LIVES, RES, RESIDE, RESIDES, RESIDENCE
ADDR	ADDRESS, LOC, LOCATION, STREET

By cataloging entity names with keyword-in-context and keyword-out-of-context indexes, we increase our ability to match or associate different variations of similar entities.

The following are a few possible variations of EMP-HOME-ADDR that could be redundant or duplicate entities.

EMPLOYEE-RESIDENCE-ADDR
ASSOCIATE-HOME-ADDRESS
EMPLOYEE-HOME-ADDR
ADDR-EMP-RESIDES
ADDR-EMPLOYEE-LIVES
EMP-STREET-ADDR
EMP-HOME-LOCATION
EMPLOYEE-RES-ADDRESS

Most dictionary packages allow a user to assign indexes or keywords to help identify data entities. However, KWIC and KWOC indexes can increase the total number of searches required in auditing for redundancies.

From the example above, let us analyze the number of possible combinations of the name EMP-HOME-ADDR.

Word 1	*Word 2*	*Word 3*
ASSOC	HOME	ADDR
ASSOCIATE	LIVE	ADDRESS
EMP	LIVES	LOC
EMPLOYEE	RES	LOCATION
	RESIDE	STREET
	RESIDES	
	RESIDENCE	

The number of words per column in the table is 4, 7, and 5, thus yielding

$$4 \times 7 \times 5 = 140 \text{ combinations}$$

If we then consider the possible permutations or different positions of these words, there are 3! (or 6) permutations of the words used in the above name. Therefore, the total number of permutations and combinations for this data entity name is $140 \times 6 = 840$.

What if another duplicate name contains more than the three words described above, for example, HOME-ADDR-OF-EMPLOYEE, or ADDR-WHERE-EMP-LIVES? This also increases the number of searches required to audit for redundancy.

From this seemingly trivial example, several hundred searches could be required to identify a redundancy. Attempting to do this with a series of several hundred dictionary search commands would be an enormous undertaking. It is obvious that data administrators must use more sophisticated tools to assist in auditing duplicate data entities. Keyword list generators and other software tools are available to assist in the detection of redundant data entity names (see Automated Redundancy Auditing Tools, below).

Auditing Attributes The attributes or characteristics of data entities can be used to identify similarities or duplications among various data elements. If we suspect redundancy between the names of two entities, we can then compare the attributes of these two entities. Do they both have the same length? Do they have identical formats? If they are numeric fields, do they have the same number of significant digits or decimal positions?

An analysis of where entities are used can also provide clues concerning the relationships among similar entities. What systems or programs use these redundant entities? In which COPYLIB or record layouts are these entities used? If these similar entities are used in an existing system, do they reside in identical positions within their respective record layouts? For example, let us assume that we suspect that elements A and B are redundant. Let us assume that element A is contained in the definition of RECORD-A and element B is contained in the definition of RECORD-B. If RECORD-A and RECORD-B are both 135 characters in length, they could be duplicate record definitions (01s). If both data element A and B begin in position 101, it is highly likely that they are redundant data elements.

Auditing Definitions If you suspect duplication among data entities, but are unable to verify this via the names or attributes, then it is necessary to interrogate the definitions for these entities. Since this is the most time-consuming method, interrogate definitions only as a last resort.

From the definition, can you identify the purpose or function of the various entities? Are the definitions of these entities very similar? Who wrote these definitions? Is it possible that the authors could provide more information about the entities being researched?

In summary, there are several methods that can be employed to minimize entity redundancy in our data processing systems. However, the success obtained from these methods is directly related to the implementation and enforcement of rigorous DA standards. The accuracy or efficiency of these methods depends upon the care and thoroughness exercised when developing names, attributes, and definitions for data entities. Are data element names meaningful? Are data elements named accurately and consistently? Do you permit both full spellings and abbreviations for the same word in different entity names? Do you permit both singular and plural words to be used? Are data element attributes consistent with entity classes or categories?

Automated Redundancy Auditing Tools

As discussed in previous sections, there can be many synonyms for any given data element name. There are an enormous number of possible spelling variations and variations in the arrangement of the words among these synonyms. This makes it difficult (if not impossible) for the data administrator to visually scan or search for the existence of redundant or duplicate data elements.

There are two tools available to assist data administrators in identifying redundancies among data elements. The tools are keyword lists and automated redundancy checkers.

Keyword Lists Keyword lists serve three purposes. First, they can be used as indexes to look up the name of a data element if the user of a data dictionary is not quite sure under what name this data element is stored on the dictionary. For example, the user may refer to a data element name as EMPLOYEE-HIRE-DATE, but the name of the element on the dictionary may be EMPLOYEE-START-DATE. Second, a keyword list can be used to identify and eliminate redundant data element names before they are entered into a data dictionary. Third, a keyword list program can be effective in evaluating the data used in existing or proprietary software. By extracting all of the data names from source code programs and feeding these names into a keyword list generator, you can determine the quality or redundancy of names used in existing software.

Keyword lists provide a comprehensive cross-reference list of all words used in all data element names. The list is in alphabetical order by the keywords (or keywords in context) of each data element name.

Let us assume that a user refers to a data element name as EMPLOYEE-SOC-SEC-NBR. However, the data dictionary name for this data element is EMP-SOC-SEC-NO. How can the data dictionary user find the desired data element name?

The data element name EMP-SOC-SEC-NO contains four words: EMP, SOC, SEC, and NO. On a keyword list, this data element name would appear four times—first alphabetically next to all other data element names that contain the word EMP, then among all of the data element names that contain the word NO, then under SEC, and finally under SOC. A user who knows this data element as EMPLOYEE-SOC-SEC-NBR can search for the name by looking up the words EMPLOYEE, SOC, SEC, and NBR. Figure 4-5 illustrates this search. The user is unable to locate the name under the word EMPLOYEE and is likewise unsuccessful in finding it under NBR or NUMBER (the fully-spelled word for the abbreviation NBR). The user then looks under the word EMP (the standard abbreviation for EMPLOYEE) and identifies the data element name as EMP-SOC-SEC-NO, thus determining that the data element is already in the data dictionary. Therefore the user need not add the element into the dictionary. Figures 4-6 and 4-7 are examples of keyword list reports generated from software available from Data Administration, Inc. This software can be used to generate keyword lists either from a data dictionary or from COBOL source code libraries (PANVALET, LIBRARIAN, COPYLIB, etc.).

Automated Redundancy Checkers Keyword lists provide a valuable indexing facility for the dictionary user. However, for a large volume of data element names, the data administrator also needs an automated means to check for the existence of duplicate or redundant data element names.

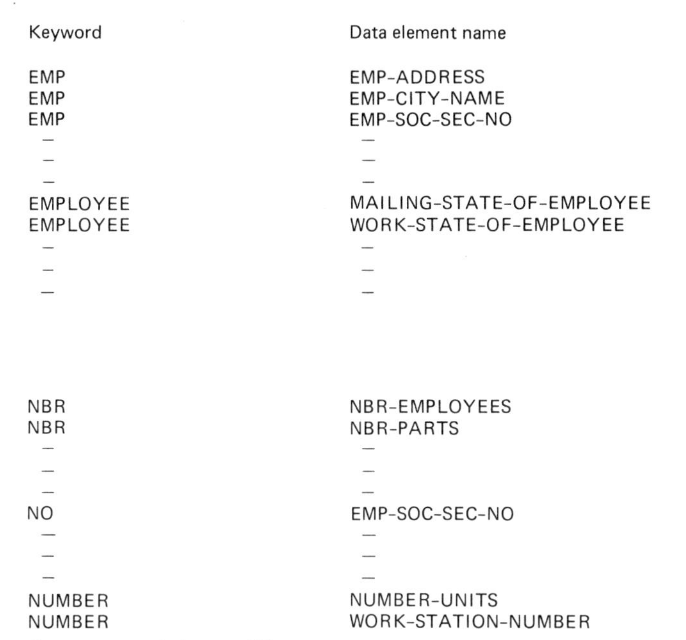

Keyword	Data element name
EMP	EMP-ADDRESS
EMP	EMP-CITY-NAME
EMP	EMP-SOC-SEC-NO
–	–
–	–
–	–
EMPLOYEE	MAILING-STATE-OF-EMPLOYEE
EMPLOYEE	WORK-STATE-OF-EMPLOYEE
–	–
–	–
–	–
NBR	NBR-EMPLOYEES
NBR	NBR-PARTS
–	–
–	–
–	–
NO	EMP-SOC-SEC-NO
–	–
–	–
–	–
NUMBER	NUMBER-UNITS
NUMBER	WORK-STATION-NUMBER

Fig. 4-5 Sample keyword list.

Most data dictionaries have some type of automated search techniques to assist in searching for the six different conditions described earlier in Auditing Names. However, data dictionary search techniques have several disadvantages:

1. The search requires several multiple, independent searches.

Example: A search for the data element EMP-SOC-SEC-NBR involves the following steps:

1. Search for all occurrences of EMP
2. After the terminal displays thc various occurrences of EMP, we must remember them or write them down
3. Search for all occurrences of SOC
4. Perform step 2, above
5. Search for all occurrences of SEC
6. Perform step 2, above
7. Search for all occurrences of NBR
8. Perform step 2, above

2. The standard data dictionary search techniques cannot automatically match fully spelled words with abbreviations for these words. For example, a typical data dictionary search facility could not detect a redundancy between EMPLOYEE-SOCIAL-SECURITY-NUMBER and EMP-SOCIAL-

KISSLIST 1 REPORT DATE = 05/11/82 PAGE 1

DATA ADMINISTRATION INC., USE BY AGREEMENT ONLY

REPORT LINE NO.	KEY-WORD	DATA ELEMENT NAME		KEYWORD LENGTH	NAME LENGTH	NO. WORDS IN NAME
1	ABILITY	ABILITY-RATING		7	14	2
2	ACC	EMP-ACC-CANDIDATE-CODE	ITEM	3	22	4
3	ACCOUNT	ACCOUNT-NUMBER	GROUP	7	14	2
4	ACCOUNT	LABOR-ACCOUNT-NUMBER	GROUP	7	20	3
5	ACCR	VAC-ACCR-EXCESS-CODE	ITEM	4	20	4
6	ACCRUED	SICK-LEAVE-PAY-HOURS-ACCRUED	ITEM	7	28	5
7	ACCRUED	VACATION-PAY-HOURS-ACCRUED	ITEM	7	26	4
8	ACCT	EMP-PAY-BANK-ACCT-NBR	ITEM	4	21	5
9	ACCT	GENERAL-LEDGER-ACCT-NBR	ITEM	4	23	4
10	ACCT	LABOR-RECORD-ACCT-NBR	GROUP	4	21	4
11	ACCT	PROJECT-COST-ACCT-NBR	ITEM	4	21	4
12	ACCUM	ACCUM-TIMECARD-CD	ITEM	5	17	3
13	ACT	LAST-JOB-CHNG-ACT-CODE	ITEM	3	22	5
14	ACTION	LAST-PERS-ACTION	ITEM	6	16	3
15	ACTION	LAST-PERS-ACTION-DATE	GROUP	6	21	4
16	ACTION	LAST-PERS-ACTION-DT-DA	ITEM	6	22	5

17	ACTION	LAST-PERS-ACTION-DT-MO	ITEM	6	22	5
18	ACTION	LAST-PERS-ACTION-DT-YR	ITEM	6	22	5
19	ACTIV	LAST-BASE-RATE-CHNG-ACTIV-CODE	ITEM	5	30	6
20	ACTIVE	ACTIVE-MILITARY-DUTY-END-DATE	GROUP	6	29	5
21	ACTIVE	ACTIVE-MILITARY-DUTY-END-MO	ITEM	6	27	5
22	ACTIVE	ACTIVE-MILITARY-DUTY-END-YR	ITEM	6	27	5
23	ACTIVE	ACTIVE-MILITARY-DUTY-START-DATE	GROUP	6	31	5
24	ACTIVE	ACTIVE-MILITARY-DUTY-START-MO	ITEM	6	29	5
25	ACTIVE	ACTIVE-MILITARY-DUTY-START-YR	ITEM	6	29	5
26	ACTIVE	EMP-ACTIVE-CODE	ITEM	6	15	3
27	ACTIVITY	ACTIVITY-CODE	ITEM	8	13	2
28	ACTIVITY	LAST-ACTIVITY-DATE	GROUP	8	18	3
29	ACTIVITY	LAST-ACTIVITY-DATE-DA	ITEM	8	21	4
30	ACTIVITY	LAST-ACTIVITY-DATE-MO	ITEM	8	21	4
31	ACTIVITY	LAST-ACTIVITY-DATE-YR	ITEM	8	21	4
32	ACTIVITY	TIME-ACTIVITY-FILE	FILE	8	18	3
33	ACTIVITY	TIME-ACTIVITY-REC	GROUP	8	17	3
34	ACTUAL	ACTUAL-PAYROLL-EFFECTIVE-DA	ITEM	6	27	4

Fig. 4-6 Sample keyword list.

```
                    KISSLIST 2 REPORT     DATE = 05/11/82     PAGE 1
                                          DATA ADMINISTRATION INC.
                                          USE BY AGREEMENT ONLY

DATA ELEMENT NAME

         MANAGEMENT-JOB-LEVEL*CD
           MULTI-MAIL-GEOG-LOC*CD
     PAYCHECK-DELVR-ROUTING*CD
                 PAYROLL-OFFICE*CD
        PREV-ST-WORKED-LIVED*CD
      SALARY-RECLASSIFICATION*CD
                  SHIFT-WORKED*CD
                   TAXING-JURIS*CD-PREV1
                   TAXING-JURIS*CD-PREV2
                 TIMECARD-TYPE*CD
           TRANSACTION-GROUP*CD
                       TUC-JOB*CD
      WAGE-ATTACHMENT-CALC*CD
      70200-TRANSACTION-TYPE*CD
                               RET*CERT-BARG-UNIT
                               RET*CERTIFICATE-NO
                         BASE-RATE*CHANGE-INC-DEC-AMT
                           HR-AREA*CHANGE
                    LAST-BASE-RATE*CHANGE-MO-YR
                    LAST-BASE-RATE*CHANGE-PERCENTAGE
                     LAST-JOB-CODE*CHANGE-DATE
                     LAST-JOB-CODE*CHANGE-DATE-DA
                     LAST-JOB-CODE*CHANGE-DATE-MO
                     LAST-JOB-CODE*CHANGE-DATE-YR
                       OL1-HR-AREA*CHANGE
                             LABOR*CHARGE
                             LABOR*CHARGE-NEXT
                             LABOR*CHARGE-PREV
                                  *CHECK-NUMBER
                                  *CHECK-TYPE
                              BENE*CHNG-DATE
                              BENE*CHNG-DATE-DA
                              BENE*CHNG-DATE-MO
                              BENE*CHNG-DATE-YR
```

Fig. 4-7 Sample keyword list.

SECURITY-NBR. Thus, to improve the thoroughness of a search for EMP-SOC-SEC-NBR, it is necessary to repeat the steps in item 1, above, for the nonabbreviated words:

EMPLOYEE
SOCIAL
SECURITY
NUMBER

3. Most data dictionary search techniques cannot match data element names whose words are arranged differently. They also cannot match a name that contains fewer or more words than the name being searched for. For example, it would not be possible to detect a redundancy between the data element names DATE-OF-LAST-HIRE and LAST-HIRE-DATE.

4. For a dictionary to identify synonyms and aliases of other names, it is necessary to identify and enter the various alias words that can be associated with each word in each name. For example, the data element name EMP-TERMINATION-DATE would require the addition of several keywords out of context to improve the accuracy of a dictionary search. The following are some of the keywords out of context that could be included:

EMPLOYEE	TERM
ASSOCIATE	SEPARATION
ASSOC	SEP
WORKER	DEPARTURE
	DEP

Keywords out of context must also be added for every entity in the dictionary. This is an extremely expensive and time-consuming (if not impossible) task.

It is obvious that more sophisticated automated tools are necessary to accurately identify and eliminate homonyms, synonyms, and aliases from our data processing systems. One such tool is DDAUDIT (Data Dictionary Auditor), which is available from Data Administration, Inc.

DDAUDIT is a completely automated one-step auditing tool that will assist in verifying the existence of redundant or duplicate data names. DDAUDIT identifies all data elements that could possibly be a redundancy of some other name. It identifies redundancies by performing a comprehensive comparison of the words in a data name against the words in all data names on a dictionary. It also automatically compares the standard-abbreviation, full-word-spelling, and synonyms for each word. It does so by matching words with other abbreviations and/or synonyms for these words contained within an "association" table. Below, is an example of a portion of this table.

Association Table

ASSOC	EMP
ASSOCIATE	EMP
—	—
—	—
—	—
EMPLOYEE	EMP
—	—
—	—
—	—
WORKER	EMP

By using this table, the DDAUDIT system can perform a comprehensive search for all words, aliases, or synonyms associated with the entity EMPLOYEE. Rearranged, missing, or extra words do not affect the accuracy of a search using DDAUDIT. Figure 4-6 is an example of a DDAUDIT report used to identify possible redundant data elements for the data name LAST-LABOR-ACCT-CHANGE-DATE.

DDAUDIT also identifies the relative probability that a given data element name is a redundancy of some other data element name. In Figure 4-8, the suspected redundant data names are listed by the likelihood of redundancy from left to right. The redundancy-auditing software tools described in this section can be used with any data dictionary/directory system. They can be used:

1. When adding new data elements to a dictionary
2. When loading a data dictionary with data elements from an existing system
3. When merging one logical/physical dictionary with another
4. When merging test-version data elements with production-version data elements
5. To evaluate the quality of the data names in a software package. This can be of great assistance in evaluating the redundancy or duplication of data in proprietary software prior to purchase.

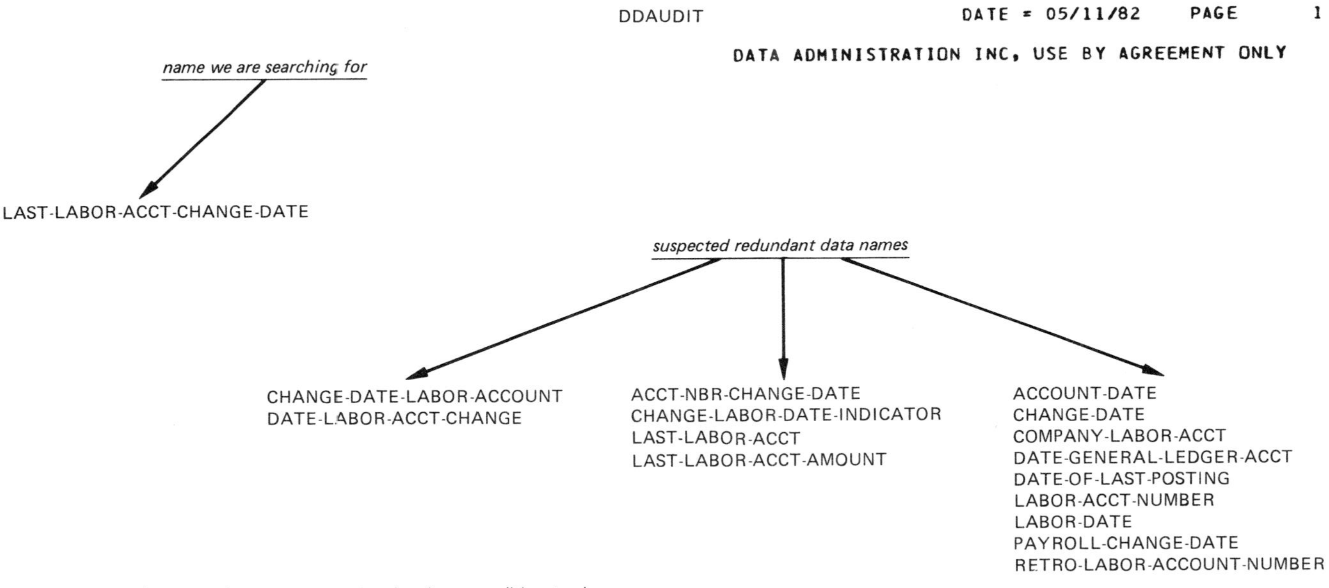

Fig. 4-8 Sample report from automated redundancy auditing tool.

THE DATA DICTIONARY—QUALITY OR QUANTITY?

Figure 4-9 illustrates the evolution of data elements during the development of a new data processing system. During the preliminary design, all data elements in the existing user views should be identified and stored in the data dictionary. Figure 4-9 illustrates this dramatic increase in data dictionary items during the preliminary design. The number of data elements defined during the preliminary design should represent approximately 80 percent of the data elements in the final implemented system.

During the detail design, there should be a much smaller rate of increase in the number of data elements added to the dictionary. During this phase, data administration will add any new data elements to support future or anticipated user views. Other additional data elements will be those concerned with system and program operating controls, auditing, and entities. These data elements include program-to-program controls, counts of data element values, counts of the number of data elements, or the number of records and segments moved or transmitted.

Once the programming effort has begun, there should be very few data elements added to the design of the system. Of course, there will be a few new data elements as a result of omissions in data design during the detail design phase.

The further into the development of a project, the more closely DA should scrutinize additional new data elements. For each new entity during the latter stages of development, DA should ask:

1. Is this new data element a duplication or variation of a data element that already exists?

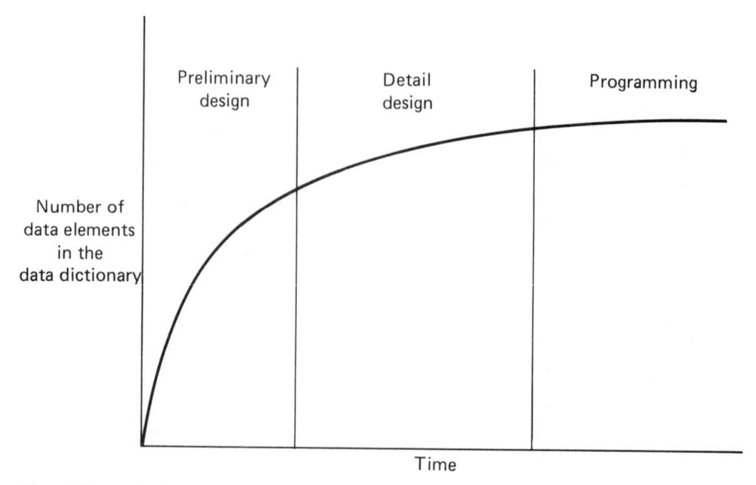

Fig. 4-9 Evolution of data elements during development of new system.

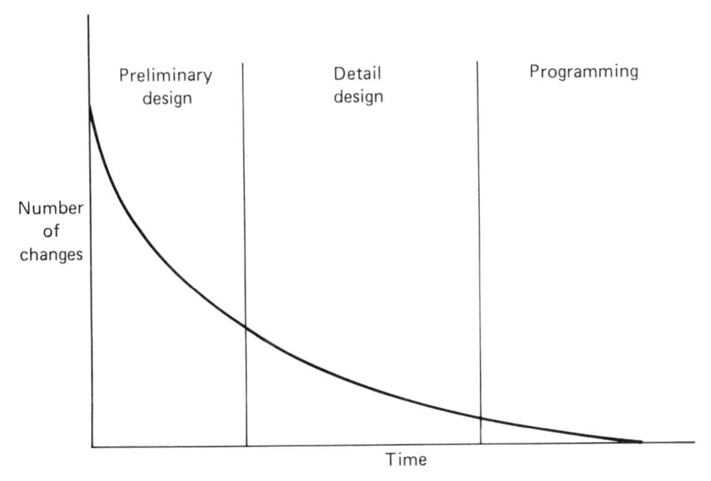

Fig. 4-10 Changes made in data elements during development of new system.

2. Why was this data element not introduced earlier in the design? Has there been a design change to justify the need for this new data element? If so, what impact will this new data element have upon existing data elements. Has this design change been approved by management?

Figure 4-9 represents an important principle of the data dictionary population during the life cycle of a new system. During the latter stages of the project, the *quantity* of data elements can be directly related to the *lack of quality* of the data design. If there is a steady increase in the number of data elements during the detail design and programming phases, this could be an indication of incomplete data design during the preliminary design. This could also be an indication of inadequate data administration control of redundant data elements introduced during the later stages of a project. Figure 4-9 represents the optimum control of data by an active and experienced data administration staff.

Figure 4-10 represents the changes made to data elements during the development of a new system. Under optimum conditions, the curve in Figure 4-10 should be the inverse of the curve in Figure 4-9. The number of changes of data elements during the detail design phase should be significantly fewer than those changes made during the preliminary design. This reflects a comprehensive review of data element design by the data processing and user community during the preliminary design phase. The small number of changes during the programming phase indicates thorough data design and review during the previous phases. This also reflects rigorous change-control procedures instituted by data administration prior to the start of the programming phase.

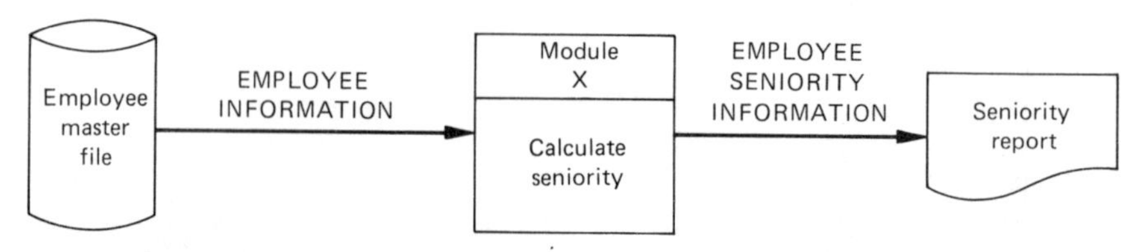

Fig. 4-11 Calculation of seniority.

DATA NAMES—PREFIXES, SUFFIXES, OR QUALIFICATION?

One of the most important goals of data administration is to encourage consistent references for the same entity. Regardless of how many programs use a particular data element, all COBOL data names for this element should be identical. While the concept behind this is sound, in practice there are problems in achieving it. The following example illustrates the problem.

Module X calculates the seniority of an employee. It reads in information from the employee master file, calculates the number of years the employee has worked for the company, and prints out a report listing all employees who have been with the company for more than 20 years. Seniority is calculated by subtracting HIRE-DATE from CURRENT-DATE. Figure 4-11 illustrates this processing.

The following data flows represent the input and output from module X.

```
EMPLOYEE-INFORMATION =          EMPLOYEE-SENIORITY-INFORMATION =
  EMP-FIRST-NAME                  EMP-FIRST-NAME
  EMP-MIDDLE-INITIAL              EMP-MIDDLE-INITIAL
  EMP-LAST-NAME                   EMP-LAST-NAME
  EMP-NUMBER                      EMP-NUMBER
  EMP-HIRE-DATE                   EMP-SENIORITY-YEARS
```

In COBOL, the record layouts for these data definitions could be as follows:

```
01   INPUT-RECORD.
     05   EMP-FIRST-NAME              PIC X(20).
     05   EMP-MIDDLE-INITIAL          PIC X.
     05   EMP-LAST-NAME               PIC X(20).
     05   EMP-NUMBER                  PIC X(05).
     05   EMP-HIRE-DATE               PIC X(06).
```

```
01  OUTPUT-RECORD.
    05  EMP-FIRST-NAME              PIC X(20).
    05  EMP-MIDDLE-INITIAL          PIC X.
    05  EMP-LAST-NAME               PIC X(20).
    05  EMP-NUMBER                  PIC X(05).
    05  EMP-SENIORITY-YEARS         PIC 9(02).
```

Notice that the data elements for employee name and employee number are duplicated in both INPUT-RECORD and OUTPUT-RECORD. By using identical names, we have achieved our data administration goal of consistent entity references. However, there are several considerations that must be taken into account when creating identical names within the programming languages.

For example, to reference EMP-FIRST-NAME in a COBOL program, you could use the Procedure Division qualification option. The following instruction illustrates this qualification:

```
MOVE EMP-FIRST-NAME OF (or IN) INPUT-RECORD
   TO EMP-FIRST-NAME OF (or IN) OUTPUT-RECORD.
```

An alternative to qualification is to modify the different references by adding prefixes or suffixes to the various occurrences of the data names. This is illustrated below.

Use of Prefixes:

```
01  INPUT-RECORD.
    05  IN-EMP-FIRST-NAME               PIC X(20).
    05  IN-EMP-MIDDLE-INITIAL           PIC X.
    05  IN-EMP-LAST-NAME                PIC X(20).
    05  IN-EMP-NUMBER                   PIC X(05).
    05  IN-EMP-HIRE-DATE                PIC X(06).

01  OUTPUT-RECORD.
    05  OUT-EMP-FIRST-NAME              PIC X(20).
    05  OUT-EMP-MIDDLE-INITIAL          PIC X.
    05  OUT-EMP-LAST-NAME               PIC X(20).
    05  OUT-EMP-NUMBER                  PIC X(05).
    05  OUT-EMP-SENIORITY-YEARS         PIC 9(02).
```

The following instruction illustrates the use of prefixed data names.

```
MOVE IN-EMP-FIRST-NAME TO OUT-EMP-FIRST-NAME.
```

Use of Suffixes:

```
01  INPUT-RECORD.
    05  EMP-FIRST-NAME-IN          PIC X(20).
    05  EMP-MIDDLE-INITIAL-IN      PIC X.
    05  EMP-LAST-NAME-IN           PIC X(20).
    05  EMP-NUMBER-IN              PIC X(05).
    05  EMP-HIRE-DATE-IN           PIC X(06).

01  OUTPUT-RECORD.
    05  EMP-FIRST-NAME-OUT         PIC X(20).
    05  EMP-MIDDLE-INITIAL-OUT     PIC X.
    05  EMP-LAST-NAME-OUT          PIC X(20).
    05  EMP-NUMBER-OUT             PIC X(05).
    05  EMP-SENIORITY-YEARS-OUT    PIC 9(02).
```

The following instruction illustrates the use of suffixed data names.

```
MOVE EMP-MIDDLE-INITIAL-IN TO EMP-MIDDLE-INITIAL-OUT.
```

There are benefits and drawbacks to each of these three methods. Below, we will discuss the relative advantages and disadvantages of each alternative.

Alternative 1: Use qualification

Advantages:

1. There is no need to create synonyms of the same data entity. For example, all occurrences of employee number would be EMP-NUMBER. This simplifies a search of programs or systems to identify everyplace EMP-NUMBER is used.
2. Without a prefix or suffix, you can use up to 30 characters to name a data element. This tends to improve the meaningfulness of the data name.
3. Since each COBOL instruction contains the data name and group name (e.g., INPUT-RECORD), this tends to improve the readability of the source code.
4. This method decreases the total number of data names used in programs. For example, this would reduce the length of the compiler cross-reference report for this program.

Disadvantages:

1. Increases the length and complexity of each instruction, and therefore takes a programmer longer to code a program.

2. Since some instructions will occupy more than one line of code, this increases the length of a program and the space required to store a program.

Alternative 2: Use prefixes

Advantages:

1. Compared to alternative 1, decreases the length and complexity of each instruction, and therefore takes a programmer less time to code the program.
2. Compared to alternative 1, decreases the total length of a program and the space required to store a program.

Disadvantages:

1. Creates synonyms of data entities. For example, IN-EMP-NUMBER and OUT-EMP-NUMBER are synonyms of EMP-NUMBER.
2. The letters or characters used in the prefix reduce the number of characters that can be used in the remainder of the data name. Compared to alternative 1, this decreases the meaningfulness of the data name.
3. All occurrences of a data element could not be grouped together alphabetically (e.g., on a compiler cross-reference listing). For example, IN-EMP-LAST-NAME and OUT-EMP-LAST NAME would not be listed together on the cross-reference report. This makes it difficult to identify where EMP-LAST-NAME is used in a program.
4. Increases the total number of data names used in programs.

Alternative 3: Use suffixes

Advantages:

1. Compared to alternative 1, decreases the length and complexity of each instruction, and therefore takes a programmer less time to code the program.
2. Compared to alternative 1, decreases the total length of a program and the space required to store a program.
3. Compared to alternative 2, all occurrences of a data name could be grouped together alphabetically. For example, EMP-LAST-NAME-IN and EMP-LAST-NAME-OUT would be listed together on a compiler cross-reference report.

Disadvantages:

1. Creates synonyms of data entities. For example, EMP-NUMBER-IN and EMP-NUMBER-OUT are synonyms of EMP-NUMBER.

2. The letters or characters used in the suffix reduce the characters available for the remainder of the data name. Compared to alternative 1, this decreases the meaningfulness of the data name.
3. Increases the total number of data names used in programs.

The decision of which alternative to choose is also influenced by the type of dictionary in which the data elements are stored and the place in which the data definitions are stored (COPYLIB, PANVALET, LIBRARIAN, etc.).

For example, MSP's Data Manager data dictionary has a facility to overcome some of the problems associated with prefixes. When producing COBOL data definitions from the data dictionary, Data Manager permits the insertion of a prefix before every data element used in the data definition. This would permit the use of synonyms (e.g., IN-EMP-NUMBER and OUT-EMP-NUMBER) and still maintain a single unique entity name (EMP-NUMBER) in the dictionary. This will allow programmers to use different data names for the same entity, yet allow data administration to maintain control over aliases. Figure 4-12 illustrates this concept. However, the disadvantage to this method is that you must make changes to three data definitions if there is a change in EMP-FIRST-NAME.

By using COPYLIB to store COBOL data definitions, you can overcome this disadvantage. By using the COPY command with the REPLACING option, you need only store one data definition in COPYLIB. Figure 4-12 illustrates this use of COPYLIB. In Figure 4-13, the data element name on the data dictionary is EMP-NUMBER. The dictionary is then used to (1) insert a prefix of XXX in front of every data element used in the data definition and (2) produce the data definition itself.

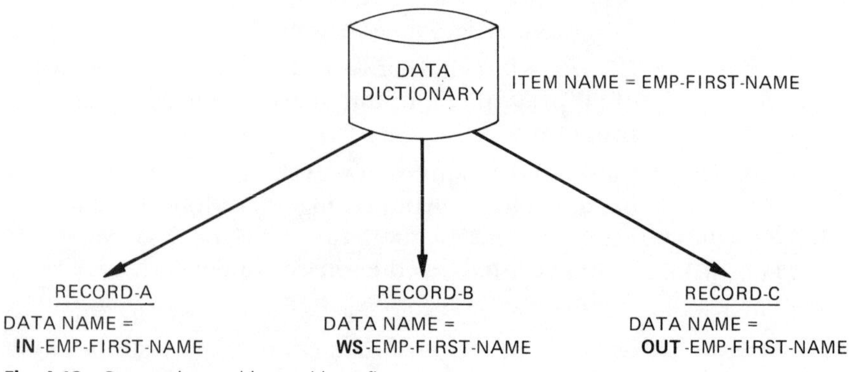

Fig. 4-12 Overcoming problems with prefixes.

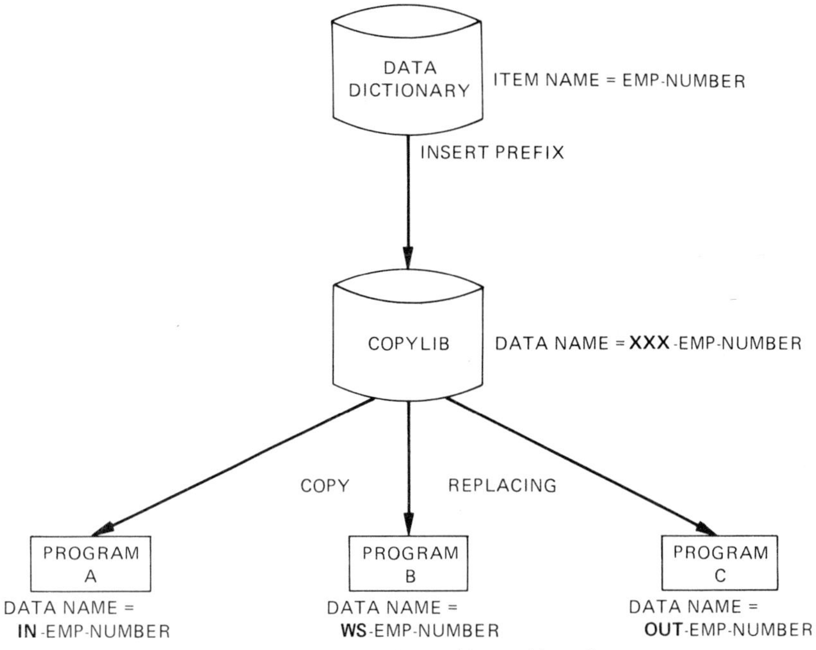

Fig. 4-13 More efficient method of overcoming problems with prefixes.

This data definition is then stored on COPYLIB. By using the COPY command with the REPLACE option, each programmer can delete or modify this prefix for use in different programs, or for several data definitions (e.g., 01s) within a single program.

In summary, there are several ways to name and reference data element names within a program. These ways are:

1. Qualification
2. Prefixes
3. Suffixes

The method employed in referencing data names depends upon:

1. The naming conventions of your installation
2. The capabilities of your data dictionary
3. The characteristics of library for data definitions within your organization
4. Your company's programming standards

MAINTAINING CONTROL OF CHANGES IN A DATA DICTIONARY

During the various phases of data development, it is important that DA regulate the changes that can be made in the contents of the dictionary. In this section we will discuss data dictionary change control.

STATUS is a data dictionary term used to describe the various development (or maturity) stages of data. A STATUS can be assigned to various logical dictionaries within the same physical dictionary. For example, during the early stages of development of a new application system, the data elements could be stored under a TEST status. During the latter stages of development, these data elements could be changed to a STAGING status. Formal change control procedures could then be put in place to control changes to the data structures involved in the new system design. When the system is implemented, the STAGING data elements could be moved to the PRODUCTION data dictionary. This process is similar to the development procedure for program libraries (PANVALET, LIBRARIAN, etc.). The stages of program development can be represented as follows:

TEST LIBRARY ⟶ STAGING LIBRARY ⟶ PRODUCTION LIBRARY

The stages of data development can be represented as follows:

TEST STATUS ⟶ STAGING STATUS ⟶ PRODUCTION STATUS

The STATUS of the contents of a data dictionary could also parallel the YOURDON progression of process design

CURRENT-PHYSICAL ⟶
CURRENT-LOGICAL ⟶
NEW-LOGICAL ⟶
NEW-PHYSICAL

or the traditional system development phases:

FEASIBILITY ⟶
PRELIMINARY DESIGN ⟶
DETAIL DESIGN ⟶
PROGRAMMING ⟶
TESTING ⟶
IMPLEMENTATION ⟶

During the evolution of the design of a system, it is important to impose controls on the changes that are permitted to the design of data. A formal approval procedure should be established for all additions and changes to the data dictionary. These modifications should be documented and filed for future reference. All maintenance to the dictionary should be reviewed and approved by:

1. A representative from the appropriate user area
2. A representative from the data processing staff
3. The data administrator

It is important to determine when to begin controlling changes in the dictionary. If controls are imposed too early in development, you will impede the development and changes necessary to data design. If change control procedures are put into place too late, this could cause inconsistency and redundancy in data use. The important thing to remember is that DA change control procedures need not be complicated to be effective. Keep change control procedures simple. Data dictionary change control procedures are to *manage* change, not to *inhibit* change.

Chapter 5

DATA ADMINISTRATION: TOPICAL AREAS

DATA ADMINISTRATION AND THE MICROCOMPUTER

The microcomputer has the potential to greatly increase the overall data processing resources of a corporation. This can be achieved by placing easy-to-use portable computer power into the majority of the labor force within an organization. With careful planning and sound management, the microcomputer can extend automation far beyond the boundaries of the traditional domain of the central data processing center.

However, few companies have demonstrated the willingness or ability to effectively manage this resource. As a result, many problems have surfaced that are directly related to the proliferation of microcomputers within large corporations. Some of these problems include:

1. Lack of information security as a result of the portability and compactness of diskettes. It is very difficult to safeguard against the removal of microcomputer diskettes from company premises.
2. High-paid executives performing elementary programming tasks or data entry.
3. Complete lack of control of the use or management of individual applications. It is difficult to ascertain whether employees are using their micros for company-related work, playing computer games, or doing contract programming for another company.
4. Incompatibility among the hardware and software of the various micros and the central data processing configuration.

5. Lack of backup support for the data applications, or expertise of each micro work station.

However, the most costly and potentially harmful use of unmanaged micros is the proliferation of redundant or inconsistent data and data hoarding.

Often, data is extracted from a central database, subsets of this data are created by a user, and the data is then transferred or transmitted to other micros. Other users may append or delete portions of this data, or save only those pieces that they are concerned with. Soon, the data is outdated or significantly different from the "master" central data. Information hoarding involves users who initially capture or create their own data files and are unwilling to share this data with other users.

Although it is difficult (if not impossible) for DA to control this renegade creation or transfer of corporate information, DA should educate management and microcomputer users concerning the potential problems that can result from the mismanagement of the information resource in a microcomputer environment. DA should spearhead the effort to encourage micro users to effectively manage and control their information resources. Whenever possible, DA should advertise and promote the use of central corporate data, straight from the "source." To encourage micro users to access and share common data structures, DA should provide users with metadata concerning the access and use of this central information resource.

THE PLACEMENT OF DA WITHIN THE ORGANIZATION

For data administration to be an effective and viable unit, careful consideration should be given to the placement of DA within an organization. Answering the following two questions will assist you in determining where DA should fit within your organization.

1. Who will be the main beneficiaries of the services of DA? In other words, who are the primary interfaces to DA?
2. What other units within the company are similar in nature to DA?

Certainly, the data processing staff is the most important user and beneficiary of the services provided by DA. Because of the need to keep a close working relationship with the DP staff, and to share and complement the technical expertise pool, DA should be closely affiliated with the data processing organization. It is therefore recommended that DA be established as a separate section or department within data processing. However, under *no* circumstances should DA be under the influence, direction, or management of application development. The reasons for this are as follows.

The goals of an application development project are generally dictated by the monies appropriated to the design and implementation of that particular project. As long as the project can be completed on time and on budget, and is of reasonable quality, the project will be judged a success, and the employees and management of this project will be evaluated accordingly. Thus the goals and objectives of application development are short-term in nature. The goals of DA are long-term in nature. The objectives of DA are to maximize the return on investment of the information resource, to minimize the duplication or redundancy of data, and to improve the management, control, and quality of this resource *for the entire lifespan of the data, regardless of application.* The following chart illustrates the differences between the typical goals of applications-oriented systems and the goals of data administration.

Systen development goals	***Data administration goals***
1. Single application-oriented	1. Application independent
2. Short-term	2. Long-term
3. Success measured by the budget of single applications	3. Success measured by the effectiveness of global data use across all applications

Thus the objectives of the application development and the DA organizations are often diametrically opposed. This is because the DA organization has a data-driven viewpoint, while the systems development organization is process- or application-driven.

If DA does not fall within the traditional jurisdiction of applications development, where should it be located? What units within your organization are consistent with the goals and objectives of DA? There are two areas or specialties whose objectives are similar to those of DA. These two units are quality assurance (or quality control) and internal audit. Does your organization now have a quality assurance function whose responsibility is to verify the quality and accuracy of new systems before they are put into production? Since DA is responsible for the quality control of data and data structure design, DA could be a viable subset or affiliate of the quality assurance department within your organization.

The goals of internal auditing are also similar in nature to those of DA. Both are concerned with the security, reliability, and integrity of the data used in information systems. Internal auditing often regards DA as an ally or affiliate in the goal of the effective use of the information resource.

DA JOB DESCRIPTIONS

No data administration project can be successful without a qualified staff. For DA to be effective, the data administrator must successfully recruit, train, and organize the data administration staff. It is important that the data administrator carefully document a job description for each of the positions within DA. Each job description should contain the following information.

Qualifications: This should contain prerequisites in terms of education, training, and on-the-job experience.

Responsibilities: This could contain a detailed description of the job duties and accountabilities of the employee.

This document will serve several purposes:

1. To assist the data administrator in recruiting the most qualified candidates. Unless you specify exactly what skills are required to perform DA duties, you may not get the best results from your recruiting efforts.
2. To provide information concerning the training requirements for your staff. If an employee needs specific training, this document can be used as justification for the training expense.
3. To provide performance standards that will later be used to evaluate an employee. By documenting what management expects from an employee, we are establishing a framework for a fair and just appraisal of the performance of this employee.
4. To provide the employer with a commitment from the employee. It is important to document what results can be expected from the employment of the DA staff member.
5. To help document the accountabilities of data administration to the organization. By documenting the duties of each DA staff member, we are providing management with an understanding of what can reasonably be expected from data administration as a whole.

A good way to initiate the DA staffing process is by developing appropriate job descriptions. Following are sample job descriptions for the three most common job classifications within data administration—the data administrator, data analyst, and data librarian. Figure 5-1 summarizes the responsibilities of the various positions within data administration.

	Data Administrator	Data Analyst	Data Librarian
Data resource planning	P	R	
Training	P	A	
Establish DA standards and procedures	P	A	R
Logical database design	R, A	P	
Data structure design	R	P, A	
Research and name data entities		A, R	P
Data dictionary maintenance		A, R	P
Data definition maintenance		A, R	P

R = Review P = Perform A = Assist

Fig. 5-1 Data administration job responsibility matrix.

Job Title: Data Administrator

Qualifications

Education: Bachelor's degree in data processing or related field.

Experience: Five to ten years' experience in data processing. Three to five years' management responsibility. Must have one to two years of data administration and data dictionary experience, preferably in management. Experience in application development and system maintenance in a database environment. Experience with structured analysis, design, and programming. Must possess strong oral and written communications skills.

Accountability: Responsible for the overall planning, control, and management of information resources to support the business objectives of the organization. Coordinates the development of databases and other data structures to minimize redundancy and maximize the compatibility of data among data stores. Responsible for the establishment of standards, procedures, and training required for the effective utilization of the data resource. Responsible for the implementation and maintenance of a data dictionary to support these goals. Must approve all changes made to the data dictionary. Responsible for the supervision of all employees within data administration.

Knowledge of: Concepts of system life cycle methodology. Structured analysis and design philosophies. Higher-level languages including COBOL. Logical database design normalization techniques. Principles for the efficient and consistent use of data. Capabilities and limitations of data dictionaries. Large project planning and estimating. Clerical and automated documentation methods.

Ability to: Prepare recommendations to management concerning effective use of the data resource. Advise management about the advantages and disadvantages of alternate data structure designs. Supervise others in logical data structure design and data management.

Human Relations: Work easily with upper management in the short and long-range planning of the information resource. Work with project leaders, data processing management, and database administration in the development, documentation, and maintenance of data structures. Work with end-user management to provide information about the data resource.

Job Title: Data Analyst

Qualifications

Education: Bachelor's degree in data processing or related field.

Experience: Two to five years' experience in data processing. Must have one to two years of data administration and data dictionary experience. Experience in application development in a database environment.

Accountability: Must interpret and document end-user information needs. Must be capable of designing logical database models using normalization techniques to satisfy these end-user needs. Must provide assistance and advice to programmers and analysts in the design of data structures. Must review these structures to assure compliance with data administration standards. Assists in the development and implementation of DA training for members of the data processing and user departments. Assists in the maintenance of the data dictionary. Provides needed assistance to the data librarian.

Knowledge of: Higher-level languages including COBOL. Logical database modeling using normalization techniques. Principles for the consistent and efficient use of data. The structure and functioning of a data dictionary.

Human Relations: Review logical database design with database analysts, systems analysts, and end users. Work with analysts and programmers in the design and use of data. Train user and data processing staff in the use of a data dictionary.

Job Title: Data Librarian

Qualifications

Education: Associate degree in data processing or equivalent.

Experience: One to two years' experience in data processing. One year's experience in programming.

Accountability: Responsible for naming and researching definitions for data entities. Must review the quality of data being entered into the data dictionary. Audits this data for compliance with data administration standards. Responsible for updating and distributing changes to DA standards, policies, and procedures. Responsible for data dictionary data entry. Coordinates and communicates changes made to the data dictionary and data structures. Responsible for generating and distributing data dictionary reports. Responsible for generating data definitions from the dictionary for use in database and application programs.

Knowledge of: Higher level languages including COBOL. Input and output commands of the data dictionary. Clerical procedures for logging and documenting changes to the data dictionary and data definitions.

Human Relations: Work with the data analyst in making changes and improvements to the data dictionary and clerical procedures. Work with the analysts and programmers in coordinating changes to the data dictionary. Provide assistance to data dictionary users.

KEYS TO DA SUCCESS OR FAILURE

The following table contains recommendations (dos) and pitfalls (don'ts) that will be critical to the success or failure of data administration within an organization:

Activity	*Do*	*Don't*
1. Plan	Plan short- and long-range goals for DA. Plan how you are going to use the dictionary. Plan the activities within DA to support the business goals of the enterprise. Involve top management in the development and review of these plans.	Don't approach DA or the use of a data dictionary hastily or blindly. Don't begin any DA project without thorough planning.
2. Document	Develop a DA charter and job responsibilities for each job within DA. Put in writing the estimated costs and benefits of all DA efforts before starting. Document DA standards and procedures. Solicit management and user participation and review of these documents.	Don't assume others understand the goals or direction of DA. Don't assume management understands the objectives and limitations of DA.
3. Automate	Automate the population of the dictionary. Automate the auditing for redundancy and compliance with naming conventions. Automate the generation of software from the dictionary.	Don't do any more data dictionary data entry than necessary. Don't manually check for adherence to DA standards. Don't code data definitions manually.
4. Market	Advertise, promote, publicize and sell the benefits of DA and the data dictionary. Invest in education and training for DA principles to the data processing and the end users staff. Devote some time to public relations with the groups that will interface with DA.	Don't dictate or force DA standards. Don't issue commands or edicts concerning DA policies and procedures. Don't expect immediate and complete compliance to new standards.

Activity	*Do*	*Don't*
5. Adapt	Make your standards and data dictionary procedures mesh with the existing environment. Tie DA standards to existing application development guidelines and procedures.	Don't expect the business requirements or company policy to adapt to your rules. Remember, with or without DA, the company must continue to prosper. Don't insist on rigorous controls and compliance before you can support application requirements.
6. Commit	Gain the commitment and support of upper management. Dedicate yourself and others to the successful implementation of DA.	Don't implement on a part time or haphazard approach. Don't underestimate the resources or the time span required to successfully develop the DA function within a company.

In any organization, the most important data administration project is the first one. The success of the first project will lay a foundation for credibility and confidence for all subsequent projects. Mistakes in subsequent projects are more easily forgiven and forgotten. Major mistakes in the first project will cause lingering cynicism and criticism of DA that will haunt follow-on projects. It is therefore extremely important to plan and prepare for the first DA project. Below are recommendations concerning this initial effort.

The first project that DA should be involved in is to provide support to the application staff during the development of a new system. Preferably, this new system should be a data-driven one. That is, it should be a system that does not immediately interface with several other in-house systems or proprietary software. This system should be a small one, certainly less than 50 programs. The duration of this project should be one year or less, hopefully six months or less. Although new system development tends to be riskier than pursuing a project to support system maintenance, the benefits will be far greater. It must be remembered that success is not just the absence of failure. To be a success you must be able to demonstrate and measure results and benefits. Benefits are difficult to measure in a maintenance mode. By carefully selecting your first project, you can improve your chances of success.

DA: THE VIRTUES OF PERSEVERANCE

The evolution of data administration within an organization often follows a cyclical pattern. Figure 5-2 represents this pattern. The

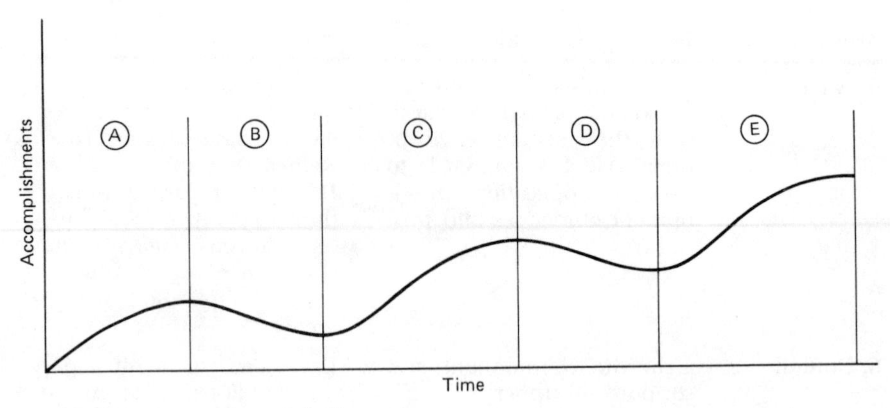

Fig. 5-2 The data administration roller coaster.

following scenario is a hypothetical sequence of events that dramatizes this pattern.

Period *A* represents the implementation of DA within an organization. As the chart indicates, during this period the data administration group makes some initial accomplishments and achievements. DA standards are developed and documented, and the data dictionary is implemented.

However, because DA is a new discipline, there is some resistance to the new DA standards and procedures. Some analysts and programmers resent the restrictions imposed on their design of data. There are violations of DA standards. This results in a higher level of frustration for the members of data administration. One staff member quits and another requests a transfer to another department. Consequently, new employees must be recruited and trained, and productivity drops. Period *B* indicates this loss of momentum.

Finally, the new staff is trained and productivity begins to increase. During period *C*, the data processing staff becomes more accustomed to DA standards. The standards are slowly winning acceptance, but there are still pockets of resistance. More people understand the benefits of information resource management. More people become users of the data dictionary. The number of entities on the dictionary is increasing.

Suddenly, an economic recession develops. The company experiences some loss in sales and is forced to cut costs. In an austerity move, some members of upper management are displaced and there is a general reorganization. The new management is forced to take drastic measures to reduce costs. Some managers are skeptical about the purpose and direction of DA within the company. Several members of the data processing staff, including two within DA, are put on furlough. Morale within DA decreases and productivity drops. Period *D* indicates this time span.

During period *E*, the economy recovers. Management begins to recognize some long range payback from DA. A decision is made to restaff DA to its previous level. Productivity increases. The cycle begins again.

This graph illustrates disappointments, setbacks, and adjustments that can be anticipated in the implementation of any new and controversial discipline. Data administration is another of these new disciplines. However, the graph also shows a slow but steady increase in the achievements of DA. Although data administration has lost many battles, it is still winning the war of information resource management.

Appendix A

GLOSSARY OF DATA ADMINISTRATION TERMINOLOGY

Someone once said: "If you are not smart enough to invent a new technology, invent a new terminology." Data administrators are some of the most notorious criminals of the abuse and misuse of technical jargon. It is highly unlikely that any two experts, or any two publications in data administration will be consistent in the use of terminology. The purpose of this glossary is to attempt to provide a simple explanation for the terms and phrases used in data administration.

Wherever possible, the following data administration terms are equated to *non*-DA concepts. Specifically, we have attempted to associate data-related terminology with system or process-related terminology. By doing so, we can create a bridge that can link the traditional process-oriented world to a data-oriented world.

Acronym A word formed from the first letter of several words (see page 39).

Alias An alternate identifier for an entity name. Usually refers to different programming language names for the same entity (see page 38).

Anomaly An inconsistency or irregularity encountered during a retrieval of information from, or an update of, a database. Normalization rules are designed to minimize the possibility of anomalies.

Atomic data The smallest component of data in a data dictionary. Examples: item, data element, member.

Association Same as relationship.

Attribute Used in two contexts in data administration:
1. A characteristic or property of a data element (see page 37).

2. In a record or segment, an attribute is a nonkey data element associated with key data element(s).

Canonical schema A logical database model.

Canonical synthesis The process of deriving a normalized data structure from nonnormalized data.

Class word A word within a data element name that defines a category of data elements. A class word is the most important noun in a data element name (see page 41).

Cohesion Measure of the independence or isolation of a data element from other data elements. Opposite of coupling.

Composite key Same as concatenated key.

Concatenated key Two or more elements which are used in tandem to identify (or locate) a record or segment.

Copy book A COPYLIB member.

COPYLIB Abbreviation for Copy Library. A central repository of data definitions (e.g., COBOL file and record definitions) and/or process definitions (e.g., called subroutines) that can be copied into program source code modules.

Coupling A measure of the interdependence or association between data elements. The amount of linkage between two or more data elements. Opposite of cohesion.

DA Acronym for *d*ata *a*dministration.

Data administration A group responsible for the planning, documentation, management, and control of data resources within an organization.

Data administrator The manager of, or employee within, data administration.

Data analysis The study of the definition and characteristics of data, and the relationships between data elements. The emphasis is on data structure, not data flow.

Data analyst A title commonly assigned to an employee within data administration. A data analyst is the complement of a systems analyst. A data analyst concentrates on the analysis and design of data structures; a systems analyst concentrates on the analysis and design of process structures.

Database A collection of data that can be accessed in more than one way.

Data dictionary A data store of information about data. A central repository and directory of documentation about data.

Data-driven Used to describe a data-oriented approach to the development and implementation of data processing systems. A system development philosophy that emphasizes the design of data over the design of process.

Data element The smallest unit of information that can be understood (or perceived) by an end user.

Data flow A pipeline along which information passes. A representation of the information that passes between processes.

Data flow diagram A network of related processes showing all interfaces between components; a partitioning of a system and component parts. Represents the flow of information through a system.

Data librarian A title commonly assigned to a clerical function within data administration. A data librarian is primarily responsible for data dictionary data entry, report distribution, and change control.

Data model A logical (rather than physical) representation of a collection of data elements and the associations among these data elements. A data model can be used to represent data usage throughout an organization (enterprise model), or can represent a single database structure (logical database model). A data model is to data what a logical data flow diagram is to process.

Data store A repository of data; a time-delayed data flow; a file.

Data structure A record, segment, file, table, or database. An accumulation of data elements used by one or more processes, modules, programs, or subroutines.

DBMS Acronym for *d*ata *b*ase *m*anagement *s*ystem. The software/hardware system that provides for the management, security, and control of the physical database structure. Examples are IMS, ADABAS, TOTAL, IDMS, SYSTEM 2000.

DD Acronym for *d*ata *d*ictionary.

DD/DS Acronym for *d*ata *d*ictionary/*d*irectory *s*ystem. Used to describe a system that is not only capable of storing metadata (data dictionary), but is also capable of providing cross-reference information (directory) about the metadata. The dictionary provides information about what the data is and what it means (logical); the directory provides information about where it can be physically found and how it can be accessed.

DFD Acronym for *d*ata *f*low *d*iagram.

Dictionize A slang term for the process of loading information into a data dictionary.

Domain A collection of data represented as a column in a two-dimensional (flat) file. A domain is all of the values for the same data element in a data structure.

Entity The existence of a thing as contrasted with its attributes. An entity could be a data element, process, program, subroutine, etc.

Entity class A general category of data which encompasses all of the data elements involved in one particular business function of an enterprise (see page 42).

Entity/relationship model A modeling technique which employs diagrams to illustrate the connections among data. These diagrams identify relationships (verbs) which associate entities with their attributes.

Example:
plane ⟶ carries ⟶ passengers

similar to the English language sentence structure:
subject ⟶ verb ⟶ object

External view Same as user view.

Field A term used to refer to a data element in a data structure.

First normal form The first step in normalizing a data structure is to derive first normal form. A record or segment is in first normal form when it contains no repeating data groups.

Flat file A two-dimensional data structure. A nonhierarchical data structure.

Fully functionally dependent A data element is fully functionally dependent on the key if the data element can only be identified (or accessed) via the entire contents of the key.

Garbage Meaningless, or unwanted data.

GIGO Acronym for *g*arbage *i*n, *g*arbage *o*ut. A computing term referring to incorrect output resulting from incorrect input. In data administration, refers to incorrect data dictionary output resulting from incorrect, redundant, or incomplete input.

Group An accumulation of data elements and/or other groups. (See page 37.)

Homonym Two or more data elements are homonyms if they are called the same thing, but have different meanings (see page 38).

IRM Acronym for *i*nformation *r*esource *m*anagement. The study, management, and control of information as a corporate asset.

Item Same as data element.

Justify As in right-justify or left-justify. Refers to the positioning or shifting of the contents of a field to the leftmost or rightmost (beginning or ending) position.

Example:

Field	***Format***	***Contents***	***Justified***
EMPLOYEE-LAST-NAME	PIC X(10)	/S/M/I/T/H/ / / / / /	LEFT
HOURS-WORKED-IN-WEEK	PIC 9(03)	/0/4/2/	RIGHT

Key A tag, identifier, label, indicator, or pointer used to locate data.

Keyword A word contained in an entity name or text that is used to catalog, identify, or search for a particular subject.

KWIC Acronym for *k*ey*w*ord *i*n *c*ontext (see page 144).

KWOC Acronym for *k*ey*w*ord *o*ut of *c*ontext (see page 144).

Lexicography The editing or making of a dictionary. The principles and practices of dictionary making. This is contrasted with the term "dictionize," the loading or building of a data dictionary.

Logical database model The pictorial or graphical representation of data elements and the relationship among data elements. A logical (rather than physical) picture of data elements and relations. Normally, the logical database design is developed by data administration and is the foundation for the physical database designed by data base administration. A logical database design is independent of the hardware or software incorporated in the DBMS.

Member An entry in a data dictionary.

Metadata Information or documentation about data. A data dictionary contains metadata (rather than the physical data itself).

Metadatabase A database that contains metadata. A data dictionary system uses a metadatabase.

Multivalued dependency A 1:M or M:1 association between data elements. Refer to the definition of relationship.

Nonnormalized data Data that does not meet the requirements of third normal form.

Normalization The process of reducing a data structure to its simplest form. Basically, normalization is the process of functionally decomposing, or breaking down into modules, a complex data structure until it is in its simplest form. A normalized data structure minimizes data redundancy and data element coupling, and maximizes data element cohesion. Normalization is an attempt to achieve the most flexible and stable data structure possible, so future maintenance of the data structure can be reduced. Normalization is the process of developing a data structure that is in *n*th normal form (often referred to as "highest" or "best" normal form). Normalization is to data as structured design and programming is to process.

Normalized data Data that meets or exceeds the requirements of third normal form.

Populate A term used to describe the process of collecting and loading information into a data dictionary.

Primary name The end user, generic, or common name for a data element. This name is stored in a data dictionary along with the programming language name (s) (aliases) to identify a data entity.

Prime word The most important modifier of the class word in a data element name. A word within a data element name that defines a business category of data elements. This category is equivalent to an entity class or a subset of an entity class (see page 41).

Process Something that acts upon data. Something that computes, manipulates, or transforms data. A program, module, or subroutine.

Process-driven Used to describe a process- (or system-) oriented approach to the development and implementation of data processing systems. A system development philosophy that emphasizes the design of process before and above the design of data.

Proprietary data The definition, format, or structure of data within copyrighted software sold on a commercial basis.

Relation A two-dimensional (flat) file or table of data elements. A table consisting of rows and columns. Each row contains the same record type. In other words, each column must contain the same kind of data elements. A row cannot contain repeating data groups. Each row must contain data elements about a common subject. For example, in the following record EMPLOYEE-NAME, CITY, STATE, and ZIP CODE are all related to EMPLOYEE-NUMBER:

EMPLOYEE-NUMBER	EMPLOYEE-NAME	CITY	STATE	ZIP CODE

The data below is an example of such a record of employee information:

01418	JONES, BRIAN	INDIANAPOLIS	IN	48309
01612	SMITH, ALBERT	CLEVELAND	OH	43216
02116	THOMAS, SUE	SEATTLE,	WA	98174
02194	DAVIS, RICHARD	SAN FRANCISCO	CA	90830
02218	REYNOLDS, PAUL	DENVER	CO	63187
03491	SAMPSON, PAUL	HARRISBURG	PA	17055
.	.	.	.	.
.	.	.	.	.
.	.	.	.	.

Relationship The association between data elements.

Example:

Association	***Symbol***	***Example***
1:1 (one-to-one)	⟶	The association between employee and spouse (an employee can only have one spouse).
1:M (one-to-many)	⟶⟫	The association between employee and dependents (an employee may have several children).
M:1 (many-to-one)	⟪⟵	The association between employees and manager (several employees may have the same boss).
M:M (many-to-many)	⟪⟷⟫	The association between employees and skills (an employee may possess several skills, several employees may possess the same skill).

Retrofit A term used by data administrators to describe the process of populating a dictionary with information from a data processing system that has already been implemented. This is in contrast to populating a dictionary during the development of a new system.

Role A particular value for a data element.

Example:
The data element EMPLOYEE-CLASSIFICATION-CODE has two roles or values. These are

H = hourly

S = salary

A role is a subset of a domain.

Schema A diagrammatic presentation. A model.

Second normal form The second step in normalizing a data structure is to derive second normal form. A record or segment is in second normal form when all nonkey data elements are fully functionally dependent on the primary key.

Sink The end recipient (e.g., a user) of data that is outputted from a system.

SLC Acronym for *s*ystem *l*ife *c*ycle. Refers to the time span from the inception of a system until it is abandoned or replaced. This time span includes analysis, design, implementation, and maintenance.

Source The net originator (e.g., a user) of data that is input to a system.

Standard abbreviation A commonly recognized shortening for a word (see page 68.

Subject data base A collection of data consistent with the entity class of an enterprise. A subject database is independent of existing application systems or organizational boundaries.

Synonym A different name or identifier for the same data element (see page 38).

Third normal form The third step in normalizing a data structure is to derive third normal form. A record or segment is in third normal form when all nonkey data elements are fully functionally dependent on the primary key *and independent of each other.* A record or segment is in third normal form when all nonkey data elements are:

Dependent on the key,
the *whole* key,
and *nothing but* the key.

Transitive dependency A nonkey data element that can be used to access (or identify) another nonkey data element.

Example:

a ⟶ b (a identifies b)
b ⟶ c (b identifies c)

Therefore, a transitive dependence exists from a to c through b.

Example:

employee-number ⟶ social-security-number ⟶ employee-name
thus, social-security-number is a transitive dependency.

Tuple A segment, record, or group of data elements. Represented as a row of data in a two-dimensional (flat) file.

User view The way an end user perceives or visualizes a data processing system. An external (and not internal) view of a system. A user view would be an input form, a screen, or a report. In YOURDON terminology, a user view is a data flow from or to a source or sink. The user view is the sum total of all data elements in an input form, screen, or output report. A logical data base design is developed from a compilation of existing and anticipated user views.

Version A variation of a data element that has different characteristics (see page 38).

Viewset Two or more user views. A collection of user views, normally as input for generating a logical database model.

Appendix B

LIST OF DATA DICTIONARY VENDORS

Vendor	*Package name*
Applied Data Research Route 206 and Orchard Road Princeton, NJ 08540	Datadictionary
Cincom Systems 2300 Montana Avenue Cincinnati, OH 45211	Series 80 Data Control System
Computer Corporation of America 675 Massachusetts Avenue Cambridge, MA 02139	Dictionary/204
Cullinet 400 Blue Hill Drive Westwood, MA 02090	Integrated Data Dictionary
Haverly Systems 78 Broadway Denville, NJ 07834	SGD
Illini Software P.O. Box 684 Pawnee, IL 62558	ADDS
Infodata Systems 5205 Leesburg Pike Falls Church, VA 22041	Full Screen Processor/ Data Dictionary
Intel P.O. Box 9968 Austin, TX 78766	Integrated Data Dictionary

Vendor	*Package name*
MSP 21 Worthen Road Lexington, MA 02173	Datamanager
Software A G 11800 Sunrise Valley Drive Reston, VA 22091	Data Dictionary
Triangle Software 2651 Kentworth Way Santa Clara, CA 95051	Pro Dict
TSI International 50 Washington Street Norwalk, CT 06854	Data Catalogue 2
University Computing Company Exchange Park Dallas, TX 75235	UCC Ten

Appendix C

CATALOG OF COMMERCIAL DATA DICTIONARY SYSTEMS

The tables on pages 190 to 195 appeared in "The Integrated Dictionary/Directory System," by Frank W. Allen, Mary E. S. Loomis, and Michael V. Manning, which was published in *Computing Surveys,* vol. 14, no. 2, June, 1982. Copyright 1982, Association for Computing Machinery, Inc., reprinted by permission.

Basic Facts Chart

System	Vendor	First release	Approx-imate users	Other products	Comments
ADABAS DATA DICTIONARY	Software AG of North America, Inc.	1978	1000	Complete product line	Revised system in development
DATA CATALOGUE 2	Synergetics Corp.	1974, 1977	250	Complete product line	Early version released in 1974; completely revised system released in 1977
DATA CONTROL SYSTEM	Cincom Systems, Inc.	1976, 1980	130	Complete product line	Formerly known as DATA DICTIONARY; Revised version released under current name in 1980
DATA CONTROL SYSTEM (DCS)	Haverly Systems, Inc.	1976	5	Variety of software and consulting services	
DATA DICTIONARY SYSTEM (DDS 1100)	Sperry Univac	1981	30	Complete product line	
DATA DICTIONARY SYSTEM (DDS)	International Computers, Ltd. (ICL)	1977	70	Complete product line	
DATADICTIONARY	Applied Data Research, Inc. (ADR)	1979	100	Complete product line	
DATAMANAGER	Management Systems and Programming, Ltd. (MSP)	1975	600	Manager products (test data, project, source program)	
DB/DC DATA DICTIONARY	IBM	1974	N/A	Complete product line	
DICTIONARY/204	Computer Corporation of America	1982	35	DBMS and related products	Completely new version released Jan. 1982
EDICT	Infodata Systems, Inc.	1976	150	Complete product line	Revised system in development
Integrated Data Dictionary (IDD)	Cullinane Corp.	1977	100	Complete product line	
Integrated Data Dictionary (IDD)	Intel Corp.	1980	40	Complete product line	
PRIDE-Logik	M. Bryce & Associates	1974	300	PRIDE system development methodology, Design Aid	
TIS DIRECTORY	Cincom Systems, Inc.	1979	10	Complete product line	Integrated precompiler planned
UCC TEN	University Computing Center (UCC)	1970	300	Tape management, direct access management, job scheduling, and others	

Architecture

System	Hardware*	Source language	DBMS–D/D System relationship	Dependent DBMS or File Organization	Comments
ADABAS DATA DICTIONARY	IBM 360, 370, 30XX, 43XX	Assembler, COBOL, NATURAL	DBMS-application	ADABAS	
DATA CATALOGUE 2	IBM 360, 370, 30XX, 43XX, Univac 1100, Honeywell 66 series	COBOL	Independent	COBOL relative files	
DATA CONTROL SYSTEM (Cincom)	IBM 360, 370, 30XX, 43XX, NCR Century and Criterion	COBOL and MANTIS	DBMS-application	TOTAL	
DATA CONTROL SYSTEM (Haverly)	Univac 1100	COBOL	DBMS-application	DMS-1100	
DDS 1100	Univac 1100	PLUS	DBMS-application	DMS-1100	
DDS	ICL 2900	COBOL	DBMS-application	IDMS (ICL version)	
DATADICTIONARY	IBM 360, 370, 30XX, 43XX	Assembler	DBMS-application	DATACOM/DB	
DATAMANAGER	IBM 360, 370, 30XX, 43XX, FACOM M series, Siemens 7.000	Assembler	Independent	VSAM or BDAM	
DB/DC DATA DICTIONARY	IBM 360, 370, 30XX, 43XX	Assembler	DBMS-application	IMS or DOS PL/I	Some modules written in compiler-level language
DICTIONARY/204	IBM 360, 370, 30XX, 43XX	Model 204 user language	DMBS-application	Model 204	
EDICT	IBM 360, 370, 30XX, 43XX	Primarily PL/1	Independent or DBMS-application	Sequential File or INQUIRE DBMS	User selects the physical implementation
IDD (Cullinane)	IBM 360, 370, 30XX, 43XX	Assembler	DBMS-application	IDMS	
IDD (Intel)	IBM 360, 370, 30XX, 43XX, CDC 6000, 70, 170, Univac 1100	Assembler	DBMS-application	System 2000/80	
PRIDE/Logik	IBM 360, 370, 30XX, 43XX, Burroughs Medium and Large Systems, Honeywell Series 60 and 6000, HP-3000, CDC 6600, DEC 10, 20, and VAX, Univac 1100, ICL 1903, Cyber 175, Prime 750	COBOL	Independent	COBOL relative files	
TIS DIRECTORY	IBM 360, 370, 30XX, 43XX	Assembler	Embedded	TIS-DBM	
UCC TEN	IBM 360, 370, 30XX, 43XX	90% COBOL, 10% Assembler	DBMS-application	IMS HIDAM databases	

* IMB plug-compatible mainframes are not listed.

D/D Characteristics

System	Entity names	Extensibility	Status capability	Comments
ADABAS DATA DICTIONARY	Fields, relationships, files, databases, field verification procedures, owners/users, programs, modules, systems, reports, response codes, user views	Define additional entities, attributes, and relationships	No status codes or version numbers	Status capability via separate D/Ds; Extensibility via changes to the D/D schema
DATA CATALOGUE 2	Element, Group, Record, File, Form, Task, Resource, Report, Module, System, User	Define additional entities, relationships, and attributes	Status codes (Existing, Proposed, Obsolete, and user defined) and version numbers	Additional entities used with IMS, TOTAL, ADABAS, DMS, OMS-1100 S2000/80, and IDMS
DATA CONTROL SYSTEM (Cincom)	User, Report, Program, System, Source Document, Element, File, Data Base, Transaction, Physical Logical Element	Additional entities, attributes, and relationships supported through MANIS	Test and production versions for the program and system entities	Entity support for structured analysis planned
DATA CONTROL SYSTEM (Haverly)	Schema, Set, Area, Record, Field, Program, Subschema	Additional attributes	None	
DDS 1100	Module, Run unit, DBA, Analyst, Application Schema, Subschema, Area, Record, Group, Data-Item, Data-Name, Set, Database-Procedures, Run stream, File, Record-Relation	Define additional entities, relationships, and attributes	Status codes (Proposed, Test, All, Approved, Active, and Obsolete) and versions (Test, Training, Production, All, and user defined)	
DDS	Entity, Relationship, Attribute, File, Virtual File, Record, Group, Item, Operation, Event, System, Program, Module, PMAP, DMAP, DUSE, Area, Schema, Subschema, Set	None	Status codes (Operational and user defined) and version numbers	Conceptual and implementation entities
DATADICTIONARY	Database, Area, File, Key, Element, Record, System, Person, Authorization, Job, Step, Module, Program, Report	Define additional entities, relationships, and attributes	Status codes (Test, Production, and History) and version numbers	
DATAMANAGER	System, Program, Module, Database, File, Group, Item, Segment, PCB	Three additional entity structures supported; additional entity types, relationships, and attributes based on existing ones	Version numbers; status facility allows partitioning by time, project, status, etc.	Additional entity types for each DBMS it supports
DB/DC DATA DICTIONARY	Database, Segment, Element, PCB, SYSDEF, System, Job, Program, Module, Transaction, PSB, DDUSER	Define additional entities, relationships, and attributes	Status codes (Test, Production, Installed, and user defined)	

DICTIONARY/204	File, Group, Record, Field, Procedure	Define additional entity types, relationships, and attributes	None	
EDICT	Element, Database	None	None	
IDD (Cullinane)	Basic Entities: User, System, Program, Entry Point, Module, Element, Record, File, TP Entities: Task, Queue, Map, Panel, Line, Physical Terminal, Logical–Terminal, Destination, Message	Define new attributes; full extensibility planned	Status codes (Test, Production, and Historic) and version numbers	
IDD (Intel)	Application, Work Unit, Program, File, Work Area, Work Structure, Data Base, Schema, Subschema, Item, User	Define additional entities, attributes, and relationships; some reporting not applicable	Status codes (Production, Test, Obsolete, Development, and Load) and version numbers	
PRIDE-Logik	System, Subsystem, Procedures, Programs, Modules, Files, Inputs, Outputs, Call Arguments, Records, Data Elements	None	One status for each of nine development phases, modification, improvement, active	All metadata relates to the PRIDE methodology
TIS DIRECTORY	System Data: Component, Edit Mask, Reserved Word, Translate Table. Schema Data: Environment, Buffer Pool, File, Environment File, Internal Record, Physical Field, Subschema, Access Set, External Field, User Data: User, Procedure, Expression Equation	None	User-defined statuses	
UCC TEN	Database, Shared Secondary Index, Data Set Group, Index Data Field, Segment, Index Data Field List, LChild, Field, PSB, Application, Job, Program, Module, and 21 more for message formatting and communications	None	Test and Production status with 256 sides	Metadata that describes an environment with IMS/DC, MFS, and ADF

Selected Capabilities

System	Maintenance methods	On-line query	Security levels	User-defined reports	Comments
ADABAS DATA DICTIONARY	Fixed format, preformatted screens	Yes	Entity, attribute, attribute value, and function (read and write)	Via NATURAL	NATURAL is a program development facility.
DATA CATALOGUE 2	Keyword driven, prompted-tutorial input, preformatted screens	Yes	Entity type and command	Customization via macro routines; additional reports via call and file extraction capabilities	New reports require user software.
DATA CONTROL SYSTEM (Cincom)	Preformatted screens	Yes	Passwords for Element entity occurrences, user password profiles	Through the Socrates report writer	
DATA CONTROL SYSTEM (Haverly)	Fixed format	Yes via QLP (Sperry-Univac product)	None	Report options	
DDS 1100	Keyword driven	Yes via QLP	Command and entity occurrence	Via QLP	
DDS	Keyword driven	Yes	Entity type, function, user, and operational status	Report options via the SELECT clause	
DATADICTION-ARY	Fixed format	Yes	Entity occurrence	Through DATAREPORTER	
DATAMANAGER	Keyword driven	Yes	D/D creation, sign on, commands, user, and entity	Customization via macro routines; additional reports via Call and File Extraction capabilities	New reports rely on the User-Interface facility.

DB/DC DATA DICTIONARY	Keyword driven, preformatted screens	Yes	Sign on, status, and entity type	Via GIS	
DICTIONARY/204	Fixed screens	Yes	Login	Via User Language	Security levels planned
EDICT	Fixed format	Yes	Entity type and others via user-defined security routine	Via the User-Defined Language	
IDD (Cullinane)	Keyword driven, fixed and variable screens	Yes	User view and record level	Customization through changing of parameters; new reports via CULPRIT	
IDD (Intel)	Keyword driven, preformatted screens	Yes	Element entity and command	Via Report Writer	
PRIDE-Logik	Keyword driven, fixed format and fixed screens	Yes	Function, entity type	Via Extract facility	
TIS DIRECTORY	Preformatted screens	Yes	Command	Via Comprehensive Retrieval Component	
UCC TEN	Fixed format, preformatted screens	Yes	Command	Report parameters	Additional security can be added via security tables.

BIBLIOGRAPHY

Allen, Frank W., Mary E. S. Loomis, and Michael V. Manning: "The Integrated Dictionary/Directory System," *Computing Surveys,* vol. 14, no. 2, June, 1982.

Chen, Peter: *The Entity-Relationship Model Approach to Logical Data Base Design,* Q.E.D. Information Sciences, Inc., Wellesley, Mass., n.d.

Data Manager Users Guide, Manager Software Products, London, 1981.

DeMarco, Tom: *Structured Analysis and System Specification,* Prentice Hall, Englewood Cliffs, N.J. 1979.

Design Manager Users Guide, Manager Software Products, London, 1982.

IBM Data Processing Glossary, IBM pub. #GC20-1699-5, October, 1977.

Martin, James: *Managing the Database Environment,* Savant Institute, Cornforth, England, 1980.

Page-Jones, Meilir: *The Practical Guide to Structured Systems Design,* Yourdon Press, New York, 1980.

Random House Dictionary of New Information Technology, Random House, New York, 1982.

Technical Bulletin #G320-6017, IBM Palo Alto Systems Center, Palo Alto, California, July 1978.

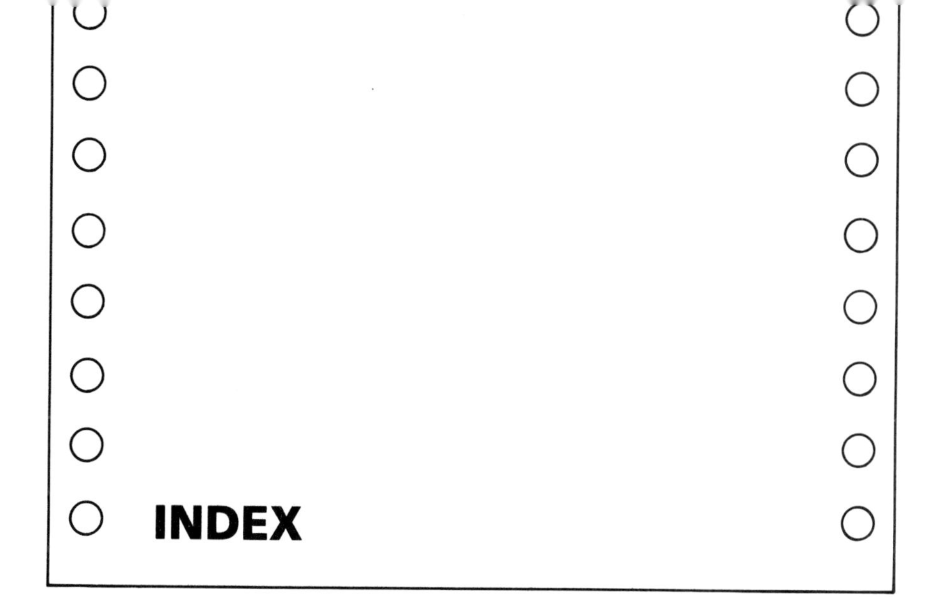

INDEX

ABOUT THE AUTHOR

WILLIAM R. DURELL is president (and founder) of Data Administration, Inc., a California firm specializing in all aspects of information resource management. The designer of several state-of-the-art software systems, he has written articles for *Computerworld*, *Data Base Newsletter*, *MIS Week*, and the *Journal of Systems Management*, and conducts seminars on data administration in cities throughout the U.S.

Sandra Schwartz